IFLIFE

IFLIFE

Bob Perelman

ROOF BOOKS
NEW YORK

ISBN: 1-931824-21-5
Library of Congress Catalog Card Number: 2006931749

For Francie Shaw

Shock and Awe language (page 9) came from web sites found on Google under
"Shock and Awe." Language at the end of Tank Top (page 123) taken from
["A Deadly Interrogation," Jane Mayer, The New Yorker, 2005-11-14.
http://www.newyorker.com/fact/content/articles/051114fa_fact]

Versions of some of these poems have appeared in The Best American Poetry, The
Boston Review, Cordite Poetry Review, Matrix, marks, The Philadelphia Inquirer,
Postmodern Culture, Van Gogh's Ear, and Xconnect. Thanks to the editors involved.

Roof Books are distributed by
Small Press Distribution
1341 Seventh Avenue
Berkeley, CA. 94710-1403
Phone orders: 800-869-7553
www.spdbooks.org

State of the Arts
NYSCA
This book was made possible, in part, with public funds from the
New York State Council on the Arts, a state agency.

Roof Books
are published by
Segue Foundation
300 Bowery
New York, NY 10012
seguefoundation.com

IFLIFE

PLOT

SUBJECT MATTER

PEOPLE

NONSONNETS

FUBAR

PLOT

AGAINST SHOCK AND AWE

(Feb, 2003)

We may not have chosen to live inside Dick Cheney's mind, but we do.

Wyoming, I read somewhere, is the safest place in North America.

No tornados, no tsunamis, no earthquakes, no monsoons, or floods. No major airport: no big planes crashing in the sleet.

But if living in Wyoming is so safe, living inside Dick Cheney's mind, though it was formed there, is not safe at all.

How do you get from Wyoming to Shock and Awe?

Getting from Love to Hate, that's easy: Love, Live, Give, Gave, Gate, Hate.

Love comes before life, and since newborns don't survive on their own, life at the beginning involves giving. It has to: breast milk, protection, language, diapers made out of whatever, some sort of attention before you crawl or walk. Everyone living was given some of that somehow.

That gets us up to Give. Gave comes next because giving is tiring. You give and give and what thanks do you get? Nothing. Or worse. They think they're entitled; they're madder than ever; they sulk in their rooms, they throw rocks.

So much for giving. The next logical step is to build a gate.

But gates creak at night, they leak, they break, in fact, gates concentrate whatever's on either side, they distill hate.

Love, Live, Give, Gave, Gate, Hate: Q.E.D.

But getting from Wyoming to Shock and Awe?

"Shock and Awe"? That's the Pentagon's initial battle plan for Iraq: 300 to 400 cruise missiles the 1st day (more than in all of Desert Storm), 300 to 400 the next, to demolish water, electricity, communications, buildings, roads, bridges, infrastructure in general. "The sheer size of this has never been seen before," a Pentagon official told CBS. "There will not be a safe place in Baghdad." Harlan Ullman drew a parallel to Hiroshima: the Iraqi people will be "physically, emotionally and psychologically exhausted"; it will be "like the nuclear weapons at Hiroshima, not taking days or weeks but minutes." The point is "to impose [an] overwhelming level of Shock and Awe, to seize control of the environment and paralyze or so overload an adversary's perceptions and understanding of events that the enemy would be incapable of resistance."

This is Shock and Awe, remember, not Wyoming.

But it remains hard to tell them apart: "overwhelming levels" "seizing control," "paralyzing perceptions and understanding."

That works for Wyoming and just about anywhere in the United States.

That's the problem with living inside Dick Cheney's mind, whether we've chosen to or not.

What's the point of Shock and Awe?

To free the Iraqi people.

Problem: "No safe place in Baghdad" contradicts "To free the Iraqi people."

Rationale: Since the Iraqi people are enslaved inside Saddam Hussein's mind, that mind must be destroyed. That means destroying Saddam Hussein's body, which means brushing aside Baghdad to find him to free the Iraqi people trapped inside his mind.

But dead people are only free in the most limited way.

Deeper rationale: It's an adult world. Shock and Awe is adult political theater for a world audience. To reach an audience that big you have to project. That's the point of Shock, the sheer size of which has never, etc. Otherwise the audience won't be struck with Awe.

What's the point of Awe?

Awe kills two birds with one stone. For the right Arabs, it inaugurates democracy, or something, somehow. For the wrong Arabs, Awe will . . . what? Awe will awe them into submission.

I can hear Dick Cheney arguing that Awe worked at Hiroshima.

But Japan was at war with us, and Awe, or at least Instant Submission, didn't work outside Japan. The Iraqi people are not only not at war with us, we're rescuing them from Saddam Hussein's mind. And as for working outside Baghdad? Destroying it will awe al-Qaeda? That's a stretch. There are more al-Qaedans in London or Berlin than in Baghdad. Maybe we should get Berlin first.

No matter how big you make Shock, you can't get to Awe.

The shocks are gigantic, disgusting, but at least they're not shocking, once we give up our imaginary safety.

The other half, Awe with its ersatz religious capital letter, we can resist.

The weapons are huge and thoughtless, but they don't deserve a shred of awe.

A small victory, but it's one device defused, the one they always use first.

THE REVENGE OF THE BATHWATER

After the catastrophe, the bathwater dusted itself off,
as best it could, and dried its eyes.

The baby, the baby. Everybody
likes the baby, *loves* the baby.
The baby's everybody's everything:
avant-garde, traditional, rhymes, it's free, improvisational,
great mimic, speak Thai it learns Thai, French French,
and it's loving, looks you straight in the eye,
no stranger anxiety, trusting, dimples, that little smile, toothless,
hair just growing in, the whole nine yards,
you like it and it likes that.

Plus it's got narrative, teleology, synergy, uses feedback,
makes friends easily, works well in groups,
grows, fine motor skills kicking in,
its resume goes on for pages, diaper bag bulging with testimonials, awards,
bursting, people calling in, spontaneously, filling up the answering machine.

All I've got is *residue*, soap suds that are so over,
shampoo long after the fact, conditioner in name only,
and the flakes of skin, perfect baby skin,
but it had to flake off because of the even more perfect baby skin underneath,
but I can have the nice older skin,
not so nice as flakes, but they're free, they're here, what choice did I have?
they're me, them and the ex-soap
and the subscription forms that fell out of *Modern Maturity*,
pulpy, illegible, the colors long gone, still bleeding.

Right from the beginning
they'd be reading to the baby, and right away
the baby's reading to itself, reads everything,
highlighting bargains in yellow, cutting out the free introductory offers,
careful with those scissors, of course it is, those fine motor skills,

dropping the leftovers, prose it goes without saying,
prose for me, no power, they say, no self-expression
unless you apply yourself, to what?
to the best that has been thought and said, printed and pissed away
in the deepest, best-plumbed baths by the cleanest, brightest body.

Body, baby, like no other,
that's what DNA is for, and history, memory, the dear diary, the blog,
and today's its birthday,
what would a baby be without a birthday,
each year the entire globe goes around the blazing round sun
at a pleasant distance so next year
on the same day there'll be another birthday,
for the exact same baby, but older and wiser and bigger,
another party but a more complex party,
it invites all its friends and they invite their friends
and it makes new friends and the new friends make friends that are new for them,
friends they hadn't known before but once they've met
it's like they've known each other all their lives,
which they have, basically,
because they're babies.

And the baby goes to the birthday parties,
and all the other babies are invited,
and they're happy to come, bringing thoughtful presents,
and there's a clown at one party and a magician at the next,
and real favors, Morris Minis to drive home in,
full of babies, each one happy to meet the others,
you have the same birthday? that's so great,
what a coincidence, you know tomorrow there's another party,
quite a few, tomorrow's packed, but there's room,
for each baby to sashay in,
waving to each other, trading towel stories,
heard them before but they're hilarious, friendly, non-competitive,
so dry you could strike a match anywhere.

And they strike them, and light the candles,
and blow them out, and make their wishes,
and their wishes come true, even the ones they were a little shy about.
What to say to these powdered bastards?

Don't know? Study, figure out what you want.
I'll be happy to listen. When they talk to you, it's always one of them,
the singular, with the face, the personality,
the quirky little style details, the favorite words, characteristic expressions,
saying, I *want* to hear what you have to say
I dropped that prose there for *you*,
in particular, the general articles, the necessary background,
no free introductory offers, not yet, not appropriate,
not till you fill out the forms, have a place of your own,
otherwise, where would they send a package?
Doesn't matter if it's free, if you can't sign for it,
you're not going to get it. It might even be oppressive, not in your best interests,
which I always keep in mind, and soon you will too.
Well, I'm late, what's new?, on to the next tub,
but you've got my email.

And off goes Baby,
clambering over the edge, the personal victory over gravity,
the signature wobble, the cute butt, dimpled like no one else's,
photogenic, dry already.

All alone, where's the revenge?
Nothing here but the old slosh,
first thought the worst thought, trying to pose as "The Thinker"
next thought a puddle around the pedestal,
and here comes the person with the mop.

Squeeze it, wring it out, dirty work for a clean conscience,
wring it into the well wrought basins, catchment areas,
the tracking systems, never a lost drop, organized,
beginning middle end, except down the drain that would be
a catastrophe you'll never know a thing.

HERE HERE

Fact: the cordially hated present
finally emerged from its dressing gown for good
the morning Proust dipped his Krispy Kreme into Kafka's coffee
and the whole market for stable meaning collapsed,
exposing me to the gravity of the moment, dinky,
but strong enough, apparently,
to pull me out of the family tree, family of man,
American consumer army family, no parachute

but the poetry map I'd stitched together
back in the uncounted days from pages flying into the future,
written or read, who cared,
here be epics,
here be epiphanies,
here be state of the art oceanic marginalities,
last month the Gross Poetic Product showed a modest increase,
continuing the trend from the dawn of history,

but now writing as I thought I knew it
has ripped open, I've gained weight, apparently,
body lurking in the weeds all the while, its endless voiceovers
more familiar by now than memory,

read by soothing Furies looking straight out at the camera,
late breaking faces making eye contact
out of the mask of uniform intelligence, brisk concern, it's in the contract,
mouths fully employed, nimble with the universal accent,
undisturbed by closeups of local carnage,
headlines crawling slavishly beneath,
we the media, all other pronouns confiscated,
and there's no way to turn this off,
the mute button's broken, like all the others,
so much for the thought that the remote was autonomous, mine,

that I could write
and it would do the rest,

this must be the work of History, Today's Date,
this morning's neural releases,
the tiny dreams,
the plans, ever-huger, are these the powers?
tangled in their tenses, entrapped, embedded, what I write,
wrote, you read, will read,
with just an is or two in between
separating making from made, broken from breaking open,

hardly enough,
but that's what there is to work with,
sirens blasting away, ignore them at the risk of enchantment,
and what's the opposite of that? and where else would it put us?
and before the question mark touches down Echo has answered,
Yes, we know, knowledge
echoes from the tapes so thoughtfully
that we know what we think

and without pause
we're back
in the loop, the world before us,
asking only for our spontaneous ignorance,
giftwrapped with gold ribbons, bows of burning desire, presents
each with a person inside,
personally monogrammed, cut, it's a wrap,
the irony will never be fresher, the studied refusals of cliche more intense,
those frames, these happy coincidental hours
with in and out on the same page,
vale and dale rolling in unison,
forests dancing onto boxcars,
autonomous trunks trundled toward utopia,

at least that's what each machined length is told
at graduation, Pleistocene entailments smoking up the scenery,

pissing away the rivers, nowhere to rest
for the weary, or the bored, or the teary,
there are no final surfaces, on earth, in dreams,
no bright pages on which to fix the just sentences,
writing on water turns out to be a play on words,
a pun that only works
because inside any language
everything sounds more or less the same,

the Federal Building
says Federal Building on the outside
and the cement is fine with it apparently,
so why, legibility wonders, does meaning have to be such a pill?
how many tons of therapy will it take
just to exit the revolving door, to stand on the corner,
amid the growing suspicion that the problem is one of basic structure,
that the mind's infoliations are only crude links
lashing the sea to its name
without prior consent, or even notice,
a kind of invasion you might say,

even though intelligibility knows it's for the best,
articulation and pleasure will follow,
they already do, don't they?
frisking around the heels of power,
but there's a certain unease, an itch
that anxious stares from even the best dogs can't scratch,
a terror that being emperor in no matter how many other brains
can't squash, no way can enough satisfaction fit inside
a single body, even if it swallows every good thing on the horizon,

novelty all day and mood music all though the night,
plus the fantasy powers, because when they give you
the keys to Philadelphia and the people who live here,
you'll find, on the same chain, the keys to Baghdad
and the bodies in the bunkers of the Federal Buildings there,
but if these keys open any line of credible inquiry then there is

no more sleep, no more awakening,
Surrealism is was
the last gasp of that logic,
its snores issuing in apnean revolt,

leaving volcanic fragments for the curators to shelve, aroused but careful,
in ever sharper catalogs, signals for the bidding
to go a little crazy, rediscover its beliefs,
relive foundational erotic breakthroughs,
but the gavel hardly makes a dent, the openings closed long ago,
the niches are decades deep, fuzzy light sifts down
on the waxy subjectivities, cooling, cool, cold,

a singular stylus would be good,
but there's only so much time to press into the material,
only so much material to go around,
which creates distortions of course, but you're not?
so amid the proclamations of perfected desire
better hold tight to your donut
or you'll be fed to the equals signs

LIQUID ASSETS

You understand the meanings of these words are beyond our control

Troops part of holiday scene as primal anxiety parts waves, paints them red

Money lines appear in scene after scene

Money shots for the unrehearsed amateurs
undressing in the unrehabbed warehouses where the plugs are full-service

Electricity is our religion and religion is Dada, across the board, across class lines,
across nation states, those ant-hills of forgotten time

No utopia is a good utopia. Not now. No use looking behind the free samples for
more free samples

Liquid assets can only be streamed

Please return to your sets

We are encountering nation states rending flesh
(you get to pick your Absolute—that's the beauty part)

A second trip to the store

A god's resume recognized at a glance. The terminator's face personal at last. Just
like last night's mirror, only closer. Not-self, exciting but xanax-calm, in the zone

The church of the unknowable election, its weapons pointed at whatever facts on
the ground, daughters sweating under the uniform

Home in the den, getting poetry from the news

We have lost the social portion of our meaning but the picture is higher definition than ever

Bunker busting bursts of hometown chic

You can enjoy the body. You can enjoy the particulars as well, creeping in like a snake into home room. You may obtain prompt, accurate motion from your muscles, and, with practice, can desire your bones to point the way they do. With practice! It grows on trees, you can't waste it! Practical!

Great second today. 33 years, a must. Other ways of doing it, in one place, in another, the same, but quite different. Nice, really. Feel the feeling. Someone has to

Same other, an accomplice during the physical demonstrandum est: the genderless goddess of

In Her will is our succession of stuttering mass positings

Alive enough to be the same old lovable chemical messages flayed alive. Something will come of nothing, diffracting its atoms until they are indistinguishable from that one stone that caught *you* that salmony September in Sandusky

I've never known a signified to stay particular so it's no surprise that they clump together in surly approximations

You hunt with the pack you learn to sniff the technical terms

Embodied ink a bit shameful beneath future legibility

Peace, people. It's all our fault, this glory, equally shared

THE CULTURE OF BARBARISM

I don't

know I

just find

myself behind

the wheel

pants on

rushing the light

something about

the past

The view

keeps peeling

back to reveal

constantly evolving

species of

pleasure and

remorse that

would make

Darwin pack

up his

little shovel

and get

back on

the boat

On our deck

they're currently

serving mixed

economies of

industrial sexwork

    worldwide crouching

on trays

    in bitesize

arrays for

    the unpixilated

collectivity masticating

    distractedly but

effectively judging

    by the

quantity of

    crumbs on

my plate

Which ruins

    my theory

that I

    wasn't totally

everyone else

But one

    thing can't

be measured

    against another

so wrap

    the ruler up

in its

    coziest examples

and then

    remember which

drawer it's

    in and

which floor

you're on

Contemporary service

industries are

no help here

autonomous tongues

broken off

to fit

the channels

and meet

demand as

soon as

it opens

its mouth

The juicers

scooters and

fanny packs arriving

in particulate

waves would

tell their

woe but

once the

box is

open only

the original

packaging remains

to spread

its rumor

that repetition

happens

You must

    complete every

field to

    get access

to a

    separate name

and keep

    up decently

close relations

    with the

body you

    started with

On this

    day of

writing my

    hand ends

in a

    pointed device

produced somewhere

    outside then aimed

everywhere to

    now appear

in mind

    without waiting

for reciprocity

It rests

    and works

indifferently in

    a single

undifferentiated state

    outside subjectivity

Maybe we

        both should

take our

        caps off

But what

        was isn't

which sullies

        even the

simplest absolutisms

Such absence

        of irony

is only

        for gods

or other

        abstractions exempt

from sequence

We pretend

        we can

but that's

        ironic—Stop!

it's saying

        Write this again!

Start over!

        Make me

be in

        another world

one without

        the torture

rooms you

        haven't let

me mention

        in this!

The whole

        language to

unlearn

SUBJECT MATTER

IFLIFE

for Jennifer Moxley and Peter Middleton
in memory of Robert Creeley

Yesterday Mina
and a world
in which she's
print and me
explaining to young fleshly class
in Lascivious fundamental times

No more erotic banter with utopian highlights and undertones of narcissism too.
That was for those who were pubescent in the post-penicillin, pre-AIDS window
framing old-fangled openness, wild oats in mucous membrane, exploding seed-
pods in civic landscape, Loy the advance guard, simultaneously her own general
and her own private in pleasure's army for the duration of the sex war. Not that
easy an army to join. It seemed somehow to be fighting on everybody's side

Then most of the day on comments. Not much interest beyond expression and
getting the words more or less right, some caring considerably less. But dourness
fades and it's part of the world

broke things
wasn't time
Hey I already *am*, I don't know how many times I'll have heard that

In 1947 or 1941 Henry Luce declares it to be the American Century, which actually
ended with the fall of Saigon, but don't tell the neocons or they'll invade Iran. Or
Syria. Whichever is closer. Or they already have. We have. Against which: what?
"Act so that there is no use in a centre." A centre? Born in Allegheny, Pennsylvania.
Go to London or Paris if you have any questions. That's how it's spelled. It seems
history is to blame

Laurence Britt identifies 14 characteristics common to fascist regimes (Mussolini,
Franco, Hitler, Suharto, and Pinochet)

1. Powerful and Continuing Nationalism: constant use of patriotic mottos, slogans, symbols, songs. Flags are everywhere, flag symbols on clothes and in other public displays

2. Disdain for Human Rights: fear of enemies and need for security justifies ignoring human rights. People look the other way or even approve of torture, summary executions, long jail terms

Then Mailer, crowded, well-dressed, reserved rows, bored, promoted, excited, Harvard book, big sexual opinions, athletes as barometers of achievement, "the King speaks to the King"

Don't waste your membranes

Being denied admission to one's inner avant-garde stung, though I was glad
Hey I already *am*
then she came
familiar with unfamiliar rhythm single use

PLEASURE

It's always a pleasure to meet Pleasure
a divinity one trades pleasantries with
always glad to see you

this time standing under
a sky half-filled with clouds

half with certain things being the case
half with anticipation of uncertain things turning certain in a near minute

certain that these days
what wants to happen will

and does happen over a stretch of time
since it needs an extended place

where you are now, where you live in fact
for the unrepeatable times pleasure fills its current shape open ended

movies projecting
good weather on bodies

not stuck in a plot funnel
moving freely under an unpressured sky coloring the time as needed

Light changing, that kind of thing

Pleasure's face is creased, fabulous, unironic
Such an absence of irony in an adult face startles

You let my look stay on your skin
while the clouds paint themselves unthinkingly with slow concentration

Nature. No, not. If it ever was nature
We can be agnostic about that

Nature has gotten dressed—cross dressed—and taken the bus downtown to
  hide out

Reader I married and was text to reading that meant the world

No need to take any of it back
run it all toward memory

where time passes
among breakable books
brokered from ear to ear with constant urgency

Pleasure is not infinite but is
waiting there, alert—you in fact, I don't refuse

After I ate up stuff from the web
I asked if she wanted to

With proper preparation (they're your feelings)
to pass the information along while it was fresh

wasn't time
cardiology a problem

Back to my cold bath
idiot food all you can eat all day hungry ghost in changing light

Taught moderately good desire
13 years basically messy
files out of date slow grab of gloom
3:06, or not. The idea is to live continuously
broke things

Why was I stuck for decades on Ginsberg's obeisance toward Pound and lineage
as if that cemented a straightforward line? A line means fall in line, take one's
place, approve what is placed in and brought out from it, shining examples, papal
bulls, balls of light. It's not easy to live a life writing, reading, talking it over, with
a sense of doing it, it's not easy to avoid structuring the whole thing like a religion.
Allen Ginsberg, old rabbinical sexy Buddhist hotshot, dying but lively, telling the
interviewer (Scorcesi? Pennebaker?) that when he heard Dylan on the record
player singing "The Time's They Are A-Changin'" he wept: "The torch had been
passed." Better the lively form-seeker, the one who borrowed from Indian street
singers (I think) ending each stanza with something like, "says Allen Ginsberg, up
the creek," up shit creek I think it was

That Notley, Dr Williams' Heiress, i.e., Alice has to make a poetic lineage is
    something else
for once and for all to not be
the beloved

Williams. Narcissism kills poems in its sleep
The opposite, the opposite

"You know that poetry you're been writing? Well, it's no good," Williams'
father in a dream, great luck

Frost, Stevens, Eliot, Pound, dressing poetry up in men's clothes
thinking evaporates as I sit down to write
(now *there's* an indictment!)

Why read X? and X?
But I'm X, too, I already *am*

Terrible early drafts
wasn't time

3. Identification of Enemies/Scapegoats: people are rallied into a patriotic frenzy
over the need to eliminate a foe: minorities, liberals, communists, terrorists, etc

there's a word for that
not every situation is new
get to some vantage and report
discriminate what moves from what seems to be staying put

Downstairs, Saturday, weather
buttered-up guns pointed in every planned direction guardians at the gates
admiring the emperor's new gas tank as he careens around in Air Force One in
    solemn celebration
annihilating all that's known
to a Diebold vote in the Green Zone

Blue Guitar Stevens uses missal and my heart sinks

You say missile. I say misrule
Let's call the whole thing off

WORD PERSON

It is as if one were a filled headline
composed by mistaking sounds
for language
falling for edges
off them

with capital always looking the other way
blinded by the searchlight of monetized desire
heading up the reorganized abyss
downsized world in backpocket

fly hits glass in early morning sun
happy as a tobacco leaf on auction day

Do poets *molt?* Stupid new sounds. Molten imagination, linking skipped association,
yes, we know, even if we don't know what or how we can hear the nouns from the
verbs. Knowledge by ear. Do I know the known? Heard it, and heard of it.
Intermittently. If sounds are allegory for social change we're up shit creek

Careful and sarcastic poetic historian
today usually runs at a frequency too low to keep track of
respectfully abusing the pre-Socratics
        the Roman imperial classic flunkeys
the innovators, ancient and contemporary
        the congratulators, the deplorers and the just plain hard workers
and a respectful shoutout to the folks back home
        kicked out of their century for no particular reason

4. Supremacy of the Military: even when there are widespread domestic problems,
the military gets most of the money. Soldiers and military service are glamorized

Modernism has much
to apologize for

but at least it's not to a higher power
People die, or lose interest

vocabulary shrivels to colorful souvenirs
of the really good conversations

SEPTA Pays Tribute to Rosa Parks
Military Solution for a City School
Trump and Croce Allied on Slots

with so many languages constantly washing over one another trying to use the
same water
you need a frequency, something stable but fast enough

In thousand year conversations like Latin, Chinese (Arabic?)
music is carefully policed if not simply sacrilized
so you only heard
what you knew
you'd hear again
though the place might be different

The medieval Church hated polyphony, the tritone "diabolus in musica"
All that *motion*

One of Pound's not-so-great characteristics
was his increasing passion to police music
Odes! rectifications! Rectifications! odes!
O immutable seasons, O resource-laden castles!
O right and wrong ways to dance!

ANKLES

Art, gratuitous self-informing rat,
pollutes the universe one more time it seems, 5:43

If you know the date
now's the time to whisper it here

For five days after the winter solstice slaves dictate to masters
hot sauce on the couch

the opposite of filling in the blanks
all to make the calendar wobble into place one more time

Heartbeat a rickety altar to the goddess of pleasure
looking good from all sides

The earth revolves
there's a lesson in there somewhere

I like that you
pay as much attention as you want in any given second

Body holding together while history
whistles past the family plot

Tenses unsatisfactory but they still seem to be existing
Words around my ankles, yours

5. Rampant Sexism: governments male-dominated, traditional gender roles made rigid. Divorce, abortion and homosexuality suppressed and the state is the guardian of the family

Running up hill, half moon on left, water on right. Creeley's "Anger that is in me like a hill": how traditional, uninnovative that sounds at first. But compared with whatsis name, bats in cave, metricist, Creeley is nonregularized, going back to Campion. Wider frame than Richard Wilbur. And Creeley is socially innovative, you can read that from early poems, he's heard and talked

Epic and lyric make their little pact under empire
There was Homer, the great sorter-out of blood stains
putting each on a slide of dactylic hexameter
so it holds still forever, more or less, wriggling
but then Sappho said no to Homer
excised her body from the clan mind
so her skin became . . . Put it this way, contact was needy bliss

But under empire there's always going to be a Virgil and a Horace, one way or another. Virgil: "Some god gave me this leisure to pipe my oat, but it does hurt to see you trudging to the refugee camp at the beginning of my first career-initiating eclogue and I'll mention you right up front" and Aeneas sighing, "Isn't it sad how the soberest servant of order has to destroy as many details as possible?" And then there's Horace

ODE

I worked on the McGovern
campaign but threw away
my shield and can't remember
     experiencing any
     actual violence

All the outer violence that brings
this wonderfully understated vintage
to one's lips, well, one is tactful
     about how one's
     corners are dented

Yours are looking exceptionally
interesting tonight. I love the
way the original paintjob shows through
     Might I check out
     that little ridge there?

Feel here in the
center of mine—a little rust
is starting. A pity, isn't it?
     Maybe we can step
     out for a spot of sex
after the toasts

Aren't you glad you live
in a shame culture?
Don't you wish
everybody did?

Pilot Evaluation Committee 2-4

6. Controlled Mass Media: directly controlled by the government, or indirectly
by government regulation, or sympathetic media spokespeople and executives.
Censorship is very common.

Cool autumnal air and sky. Its insistences seem so doctrinal. Adorno: "The barter principle, the reduction of human power to the abstract universal concept of hourly wages . . . imposes on the whole world an obligation to become identical, to become total

But money is the great unequalizer

I'm down. A-fib

actually be thinking and writing one motion. As opposed to: what to *work on?* What to say?

Heavy therapy. A labor to speak. And now to move fingers to type. Can't call up the feel of being loved by my mother, which is hard is it not

Leo Steinberg, *Other Criteria*, demolishes Greenberg's modernism revealing the dull machination in the drafty backroom where Greenbergians went to put on their robes for the flatness canticle (not that paintings weren't getting flat then): "The distinction a critic makes between Modern-self-analytical and Old Master-representational refers less to the works compared than to his own chosen stance—to be analytic about the one and polemically naive about the other"

One can think of contemporaries here: Ron's SOQ. But careful reading is a weak implement to shake apart the binarism of such judgments. Close readings mostly aren't interesting to read: the demonstrations always having to increase geometrically. Eventually, with however much good will on the reader's part, you run out of attention, room, time

But doesn't every word count? And every shape matter? Aren't some poems better? And isn't there something systematic about judgment? Aren't there sides?

I haven't solved the problem of being

Put ideal typing there I suppose

Practicing sloppy years, not know, really, where? Ridiculous

None of this remains visible, only legible

chronological pep talk. And as the little hut was the terminus of existence, that really can benefit more than just my own ego streamlined on the page

Yesterday formally answered questions from Childhood
Ate a yolked spell that long evening, not having forgotten to *Pun*. Bucked off and hung lively going unthonged to the hounds—seven-league boots of *Gone*, pelt out and paws wet. It was about time in writing, getting even in some minutes odd in others. One last chance for the *Past*

July *early*, earlier than what
Dream reading cut off

familiar head upon waking. Torso in same? Accumulations in place?
With a flunking motion pushes pillow back to prior dark

two small scraps

Finishing *Jude the Obscure*. Hardy's sentences are *fantastic*, crisp, tragic, elaborate, prompt and funny. Is contemporary prose, New Sentence, high theory, jumping fragments, as vivid, word by word? It's a phenomenological question: ordinary brain pharma. Pragmatics of breathing while reading underlies all that's vivid in writing

Reader is flesh and blood
writer is flesh and blood
—what's with all this mediation then?

To library for beautiful Scarlatti sonata heard through scratchy radio static at Valley Green this A.M. where I watched 5 inches of yesterday's rain in the creek then ran alongside. Little Father Time has just killed himself and the younger children: "Done because we are too menny." Mean corny truth-pushing plot-meister. Meanwhile, reading the editorial notes prefacing *Così Fan Tutte* and *Don Giovanni*, magical scores but I can't actually animate the sound. (The viola's C-clef, etc.) The editor, who shall go nameless here, concludes both his little statements with the time and place of their utterance: Berlin, Summer, 1941

all day later, nothing

We're all extra now
Agreed? Philadelphia, Winter, 2006

Oppen: "I think we would all like Sandburg to be a better poet than that crew
[Pound, Eliot, Yeats, seen as reactionaries]. He just so obviously is not.—add
Joyce, Proust, Lawrence for that matter. Leaves Rezi and Williams. Both of them
basically democratic, in spite of Rezi's nationalism, and Williams' sense of aristoc-
racy—his simple, asinine H. L. Menckenism once in a while. But when it's good
it's really almost classically American-democratic.—AND being democratic has
got to be absolutely non-dogmatic, a-political, unsystematic whereas system, dog-
matism and all the rest is found tolerable in Yeats Pound Eliot"

Can't *see* a primary layer of color in Pollock and *somewhat* similarly
there's no way to find a basic frame in Paterson
With Pollock you can hardly see the complex overlay but it registers at once
With Paterson you have to grasp at it backwards, but after 3 or 4 or 5 tries
ordering seems reductive

[Quixotic analogizing. I'm just trying to make them *be friends*]

Avant-garde is middle-aged, but romanticism is forever young. Dorian Gray

Modernism's combover

Spicer is a ghost longing for actual flesh and blood. Somebody else's hopefully

Wood-thrush song, footsteps, panting

Wood-thrush song, footsteps, panting

So, learn to touch type for fuck's sake. Organize. Clear off work surfaces. Learn
where the keys are, where your fingers are, whose

The non-elected present declares
"I'm the war god"

no ethics, only miracles, broadcast obedience
and a seemingly inexhaustible supply of bombs in the jam closet

Uninsured bastards behind excellent gunsites
shooting at the poster of the primal father
Exhausted pricks patrolling the head of a pin

retailed humiliation, private shaking and audience guffaws, breaking ribs with hysterical
release, because wholesale humiliation bulldozed what once was home (sold at
employee discount plus a decent profit for self-proclaimed mediocre golfers)
(smile, explode, cum in easily downloadable shots). But home is impossible to
reach, and decoding the mean another interminable job, putting electrical impuls-
es, salts, fat, bone and will on hold

awaiting historical
recompense for stolen homeland
(but that's the wrong word)
capital h Hell to pay
and in that situation
labor never gets paid
Children's armies over the cliff

It was dark needless to say. And as I go to write this, again, it is dark. Of course,
if it never got light in between sessions of dark, then "again, it is dark" wouldn't
have much bite. And if you never wake up between dreams then they're hardly
dreams now are they?

Really all this is to apologize for the poor visibility, the disgusting state of the media

EVERYTHING THEY TOLD FREUD TO SAY

There was an imbalance. I
was sleeping but they were there

and even though
dreams can be in bed

I was outside
at some indeterminate close difference

to the bed, as I said,
all other embodiment remaining occluded

7. Obsession with National Security: fear is used as a motivational tool by the government over the masses

8. Religion and Government intertwined: regimes use the most common religion to manipulate public opinion. Religious rhetoric and terminology from government leaders, even when the tenets of the religion are opposed to the government's actions

Back from Orono
factor in masculinity
kinds of marks
enthusiasm, sentimental & naive

In theory ahistorical power shouldn't be possible but "it works every time"

Williams, Thomas Hart Benton. Stein, . . . rhythm . . . rhyme (microphone too low)

in bed, 4:45, birds, grey outside, thought what if she suddenly wakes up very amorous. Mentioned this at breakfast and she found it tedious. Give. Reality. A. Break. (GRAB) Thinking: amorousness a kind of fantasy to share, and then poetry, shared fantasy? How physical? Ratios, tipping points, pleasure

Romanticism: Poetry and Sleep
Modernism: Wake up. *Finnegans Wake* isn't supposed to put the reader to sleep

"Only H. and M. did anything of interest"
Do you have to connect that up with *Propertius* or *Cathay*?
Or with the editorial and literary interventions?
Didn't Pound do "things of interest" besides making a fascist and a fool out of
  himself ?
Aren't there lines to be drawn?

To have, with enthusiasm, knocked
that a Mussolini would open

Erased: but it had to do with the line in Pollock
(not bounding shape, simply a gesture of
opticality) and in Williams, not totally
different, with inside and outside perpetually shifting

1:43. Williams article so I can write Pollock WCW piece and work on semidone
poems. A-fib; just me. Why do this?—but am doing it: 1:44, 652 words. Trollope
wrote with his watch in front of him: 250 words every 15 minutes. Now forgotten

Williams thought he
was

doing something of
what

Cezanne did. "This
Madam

seems to be
paint"

Knowledge built out
of

singular, equivalent units
Scraping

words clean, et
cetera

But in Pollock's
case

what are the
units?

9. Corporate Power is protected: business aristocracy puts the leaders into power, creating a mutually beneficial business/government power elite

Trying to sort 2crit subdirectory, 1crtbook. Feeling affection for laptop as I type and drag. Here's birm.wpd 23000k, but here's asphodl.903 39000k

SAPPHO, BE

There is only one love

    I love myself more. Sappho loves

       her own

   hateful mirror

all, a second choice, you

Asphodel is modernist solstice? Bring a picnic. Eat it on the grounds

Finally found psu2.o99. The confident optimism that emanates from "The New Spirit and the Poets" is still a pleasure, especially if one filters out Apollinaire's rictus-like French nationalism. Poetry, in his vision, will make use of all manner of formal devices, avant-garde or no: rhyme, free verse, typographic experiment. It's not competing with the other arts, but is buoyed by nearby progress. Apollinaire imagines future artists with access to the "entire world, its noises and appearances, the thought and the language of man, song, dance, all the arts and all the artifices . . . . a liberty of unimaginable opulence. Today the poets are serving their apprenticeship to this encyclopedic library." The internet, we might say now

Asphodel and the Pisans. Crisis poems of lifetime modernists who've been run off the road by modernity or however you want to designate change too rapid for anything but passive, accidental registration. Modernity has torched claims of modernist control, 'design,' even tho Williams claims to harness the A-bomb.

While Asphodel was being published the H-bomb went off, the Rosenbergs were executed. H.D.'s *Trilogy & Helen in Egypt*: crisis-poems. There when we need them. The ambulance showing up within a decade. Their and our happy ending. Like finding a linzertorte in the picnic basket in the mental hospital grounds. Ginsberg turns to religion for a name. Moloch. Irony, used without irony

Hoaxes. Duplication of the nonextant. Who put the re- in really?

Dan Savage wingnut sociopath improvising his show. He says he has an orgasm fantasizing jets overhead flying to bomb Damascus. A comedian. Does it have to be improvisation, he can't actually consider the consequences? All improvisation based on the certainty of the self-hidden individual, incomplete until the current splash into perfect embodiment? The applauded improvisation—*Lavender Mist*— proves the trans-all-value of the self, not formed till that moment

10. Labor Power is suppressed: because power of labor is the only real threat, labor unions are eliminated or suppressed

        painted for the ruling classes
    middle class could pretend (*National Geographic*)

proletarian portraits
        almost kitsch.   not kitsch at all
makes his stuff himself, out of all the others
                "too depressed to get out of bed" confirmed

No mother there, scraps of memoir around Stendhal

glamorous earthlings
children eat what you cook
court what you see

Smitten, lighten, eaten

Namuth movie and outtakes show Pollock an obsessive compulsive. "He is working for Ford, doing his best for Vilet de Laszlo. . . . 'automatism' looks finally more like robotics than shamanism." Beauty "in the face of surveillance and de-skilling."

Namuth was the foreman, enraging Pollock

The Dadaists down to Burroughs, the more revolutionary recombiners and destroyers have, I think, faith in the inviolability of the already-given individual word. So they are, in fact, conservative. They want to conserve those words; they're not making new words . . . But that's not true because gadji beri bimba etc. So that's wrong. Maybe just Burroughs

Genealogy only goes backwards, getting singular. Going back to the great genie, putting the genie back into the genealogy. Portable, around your neck. Rub as needed

Learning is a highly structured infectious fantasy with very strict rules that are always being broken, some times more than others. Poetic learning, the Vortex, Translatio Studii: school of Paris, then school of New York, school of San Francisco, school of Philadelphia, drifting forward in one big sticky dream. All history in one diaphanous head, patting itself on the back, as per usual. One place, where prior learning has been absorbed, and is now, by existing again, made different. Particles of water going up and down; waves going forward, crashing on tumbling pebbles. Totality of the ocean, hypnotizing the fish. The great globe of being. You had to have been there

THE PAST IS NO PLACE FOR SOMEONE LIKE YOU

I read it in a book, a big one
about an interesting person, very—
but I am not those decades

how Andy Warhol presented Frank O'Hara
with a drawing of his penis at a party
Frank O'Hara's penis, but not Frank O'Hara's party
it was a party where uptown curator Frank O'Hara did not smile upon his
    represented penis
commandeered—in a virtual sense—by downtown upstart Andy Warhol

never smiled until Pittsburgh Andy began making it everywhere, which is where
here wants to be too

Where is that drawing now, the venal sun wonders
and where is that smile
and the wagging tails of yesteryear?

All I'm saying is remember I exist
That's all each tail wants

It's not that I don't like the decor particular to my contemporary situation
or at least recognize it
or sit in its midst at any rate

it is that any decor problematizes
the system of rewards
administered by oneself
– but no one seems to know precisely how this is done –
in one's momentary upskirt monastery droning continuity
we like to call our time
love to
engaged in one's objective and one's subjective stirrup
during one's there-I-could-never-be-a-person displays of horsemanship
streaking into the earnestly timed close of the latest day
with its streetlight-softening moonrise
bricking and unbricking the living arrangement
doled out dolled up in words my dear, words, phrases, they make you look so great
Hold it, just like that

You can exhale when you're dead

We are a long way
from Frank O'Hara's penis
but not from the question of success in the art world
advanced just beyond market regulation, conducive to no single civic happiness
just over the edge of closely desired public statement and its narcoleptic negotiations
but there are so many timeshares
and barely systematic dreads
scenic overflows of utter legibility
that at some point just about everyone's lips are paralyzed with grief

over the despicable pictures
hardly to be assuaged by the so-called writing H. D. saw on the wall I read of in
   a book
another big book
about another interesting person, very—
and this time the book was interesting too—

But the wall is still wall

Or is it always just school, and then the swimming pool?
Where Keats wrote his odes
Drugstore bathingsuit
Byron laughing at his boner
Later, on the bottom, turning blue, leave him
Bodies turning out separate

11. Disdain for Intellectuals and the Arts: open hostility to higher education, and
academia. Professors censored or even arrested. Free expression in the arts and let-
ters openly attacked

moist & sunny. Up to the bridge, colloidal pouring water surface, not a whirlpool,
no vortex, but some living confluence of days. Pleased. On the way back I saw a leaf

Literary generations. Is Wieners Olson's son? Is Bishop Moore's daughter? And
then O'Hara begat Berrigan? So the whole thing looks less and less likely.
Berrigan's hoax-interview with Cage where the mother's supposedly lying naked
on top of Cage tied up underneath. Chance was in control from then on. Chance
gives birth to what? Particulars?

Rauschenberg more the begetter of *The Sonnets* than O'Hara

To historicize Warhol now and to transplant a hydrangea successfully, roughly
equivalent tasks. A dandy (Whistler, Manet). Wanted to be as famous as the
Queen of England; dissed Siquieros: "just action paintings. Anyway, Pollock was
much better. I wish I had a Pollock." Victims: "I wasn't sorry for them exactly. But
people go on their way and they don't really care if some stranger just got killed.
So I thought it would be nice for those unknowns to be thought about by those

people who would never normally do that"

12. Obsession with Crime and Punishment: police are given almost limitless power to enforce laws. People are willing to overlook abuses and even forego civil liberties in the name of patriotism

Can't teach everybody, not everybody wants it. But deep down incorrigible thinking that I have to: poetry is Homeric, something everybody hears. As opposed to what? Administer your branch

Pound the news broadcaster. In 1912 he broadcasts news of the Parisian schools via Imagisme. In 1915, he broadcasts news of China via *Cathay*. In 1919, he broadcasts news of Japan via Noh plays. But in Rome when he's finally behind an actual microphone he's a paranoid hysteric (the double whammy) who thinks he's the news

news of Greece via "Papyrus" and of Rome via *Propertius*. "Papyrus": the news from Greece is that the news is hidden. For H. D., the news from Greece is that the news has been censored for millennia, but is present and vivid

"Your poetry's no good": end of the triumphal archway, no more staring as the commandant's statue drags Don Giovanni to hell every night except Sunday, twice on Saturdays

NOW CALL IT A POEM

Fools have big bombs, relatively cheap, and somebody
should issue a recall for the personal pronouns

they're guaranteed for life but as you can tell as well as I
shuffling in a direction, head attached, backwards

what I most wanted to avoid
blew me apart, for some reason

never quite real before, but now more than real
so much for continuity

fatal error
limbs scattered

having gone back and removed the asterisks marking separation
it's now one differing piece stitched
together like in old scribal nospacesbetweenwords days

To move, to please
to end up knowing what you know in the present

Awoke a few times before getting out of bed at 5:50. Getting dressed to go run-
ning, I sat on the green chair and saw the VCR say 5:50, my clock radio say 5:51,
and thought of the new clock radio F got for the bathroom which must also be
declaring it to be 5:50, give or take

Formalism can connect features in a poem to features of prior poems but the for-
malist can't account for change and finally has to invoke the evolutionary weath-
er fronts, Romanticism, Modernism, Postmodernism. The cultural critic has an
easy time explaining change: the art activity slides on historical forces like boul-
ders on a glacier. But don't say glacier or evolutionary weather fronts unless you're
a nature lover. Stages of material development

Is poetic knowledge something that someone else can also know? Or is it strictly
confined to the poet's body?

Fighting off bad old
Glum and destroyed the vacuum before I retroactively constructed the 'nice guy'
    residue
By Saturday night I only felt a verbal memory, fatigue, and suspicion that some-
thing still exists down there. It's not quite bobbing for apples (and I note the "bob"
there) but that my efforts to grasp the thing push it away, like trying to retrieve a
submerged block of ice on the shore of a large cold lake in darkness (Ice floats,
but this ice is only semi-buoyant.) (And I note the submerged "boy")

The point is writing

Erase that

13. Cronyism and Corruption: the regimes are governed by groups of associates who appoint each other to government positions and use governmental power escape accountability. National resources appropriated by government leaders

14. Fraudulent Elections: sometimes elections are a complete sham. Other times, they're manipulated by smear campaigns, assassination, legislation to control voting numbers or boundaries, and manipulation of the media. Typical use of judiciaries to control elections

At the sound of my voice I wrote voiceover
the debris is real enough

Bris—what did Louis Kahn's cousin the Rabbi say about brises? My memory has
  been nicked.
They can't take that
away from me, the old son says, the old *song* says
mix them and both suffer

so there's *no way* to learn anything?
              just drift around on lacy jags of meant stuff
                        and see who you meet?
A nonce form: the premise is that history is always new, that forms reflect its
authentic newness

tradition always ending, repetition failing, failing

        Tityrus: OK. Triumphalism of *what*? The avant-garde?
        Daphnis: Not the avant-garde but the idea of the self-righteousness of the
experimental alternate tradition to the
        Tityrus: It's truly innovative, genuinely new
        Daphnis: Yeah, that we're finding a form for the moment
        Tityrus: And the moment is new
        Daphnis: So when Lycurgus steals, writes a poem in the exact same form as
the one poem that Thyrsis wrote in that form, so there's only two poems extant
that are in this form, one written by Thyrsis which Thyrsis presumably thought
would be a nonce-form, and one written by Lycurgus in which he absolutely
        Tityrus: He mimics it perfectly, like Zukofsky and Catullus

Daphnis: Except with this British content, right? Which is totally different than the Thyrsis poem. So it's no longer a nonce-form; it's been codified. And that's what I'm saying about Language

Tityrus: And suddenly novelty becomes historical

Daphnis: That the gestures that Language poetry triumphantly says are still radical are actually super-codified now. And that's my whole point. We need to rethink that equation

Corydon: This sounds like Libbie Rifkin's take on Menalcas and the way that Menalcas was writing Frank O'Hara poems or John Ashbery-like poems and taking lines and phrases, or making his own very very close imitations. And doing it in the spirit . . . And I think Lycurgus is a little bit like Menalcas

Tityrus: It's like Pierre Menard because to actually take somebody else's lines is to do the polar opposite of what O'Hara does. If O'Hara wrote a line, that's one thing

Daphnis: Intense worshiping of

Tityrus: But worshiping is a distorting activity

Daphnis: But with Lycurgus and Thyrsis, and O'Hara and Menalcas . . . Menalcas is like, I can kick his ass. I can write a better O'Hara

Tityrus: Is it I can kick his ass or I can be him. Oh be Thou me! West wind

Daphnis: I can beat him in the ring in his own game, basically

Tityrus: But he *can't* because he imitates him

Daphnis: If you have a character-based or a personality-based poetic, then it's impossible

Tityrus: Then you've lost before you start

Corydon: Menalcas and Lycurgus are quite alike in personality, both being wordsmiths, they're utterly brilliant in the handling of language

Tityrus: Or in the handling of literary historical materials

Corydon: Exactly. They're very very aware of the literary tradition, and so . . . it's like virtuoso pianists. They're playing somebody else's work. It's only possible to be Rachmaninoff, at the beginning, within a tradition

Daphnis: In some cases, too, it's premised on amnesia

Tityrus: The audience's? or the poet's?

Daphnis: The poet's. Finding your way to obscure writers who . . . For example, Thyrsis at the *time* . . . Now it's very different. Some of the poets that Lycurgus chose to fetishize: Damoetus. No one knows what Damoetus sounds like, except for a tiny percentage, so he could become an exact imitator of this person in a British context and there's no memory of that

Tityrus: It'll seem like originality . . . to the benighted

Daphnis: Right, exactly. It's like the situation where someone finds Menalcas and says, Wow! This is really interesting, and you say, well have you read O'Hara. Who knows what order it'll come in later. You know it's like that moment when you first . . . whoever

Tityrus: Well, name somebody. Anybody. Roethke

Daphnis: Or Shakespeare

Tityrus: Oh, OK: better

Daphnis: Or even Dante. Then you read Virgil and it's: Oh, OK. That's where he got that and that's where he got that. You piece it back all out of order

Tityrus: OK, here's the thing. Is originality, the fact that Virgil did this first, more important than . . . . or is the fact that here is a *form* that's historically and culturally portable. And that *that's* what's good. Virgil could do it and since Virgil discovered it we'll give honor to Virgil *but* Dante can use it without any blame and it shows how virtuous the *form* is. It doesn't show how venal Dante is, but how efficacious

Daphnis: It's the gymnastic parable. This is the only thing I have to compare it to: in gymnastics you have a move. And 12 gymnasts all do the same set, they have to do this twist and that twist, and this jump and split. And everyone comes on and does the exact same series of formal gestures. But one can judge this person's use of the formal gestures as opposed to that person's use of them, and how the interpretation of a very codified or a very strict set of formal gestures. That's why form in poetry

Tityrus: OK. Here's the big question: to use gymnastics as the frame, that cedes the power to the judges, who are the experts. Now is poetry like gymnastics, in terms of awards, in terms of quality

Corydon: I think it's interesting that Thyrsis came into the conversation. Because I think that we don't observe enough that in darts or in gymnastics it's possible for someone to be an innovator, who shows you a new way of making the moves, that they themselves might not take very far. And I would say that Thyrsis is an astonishing figure because he makes possible the careers of about ten other poets. Bruce Andrews is only possible because of Thyrsis. And for me that's not a negative judgment on Bruce Andrews's work, which I find very powerful. But it comes straight out of some of the Thyrsis work of the late 60s and early 70s. Thyrsis shows you how you can do it, but he usually does it in a limited sphere. He's very restless. And he's not an author who goes toward . . . I don't know what to call it: personal insight

Tityrus: Social depth. Watching TV
Daphnis: It's really sociologically
Tityrus: Now I'm going to use this as my statement tomorrow
Daphnis: OK, I'm shutting up

AUTONOMOUS WRITING TIME WITH QUOTE

mm/dd/yy remains on the alert trying to read Shakespeare's brain but it's slow going, with each attempt taking us farther away from any self-serving bones

Cognitive science does have things to say to playground bullets circumcising the split subject, and can rescue a diffuse but real enough sense of accidental agency, which, even if 2% accurate, is enough to fatally contaminate a person's empirical bathwater. The sloshes provide some sense of motion between the ears, never forgetting the communicating vessels between legs, thus one stoops to be conquered by unconscious syntactic tactical groups, literate messengers repeatedly tearing back to report a sense of language as "profoundly alienating, but mine own"

The way children of pidgin speakers form creoles is the way writing reads, marking undetermined numbers of pixels per conscious exhalation

But Gombich is right: that face you or I see in the mirror is half size.

Remember when it all meant? It hardly seems fair that we, the so-called human element, were little more than carrots at best, diced into history, kept on the boil by lofty archaic prayers from a range of severed heads, none of which was remotely ours. There was money (but no benefits) if you could learn the programming to keep them circulating fast enough. Otherwise, go home, or homeless, breakable at the slightest smash

George says "up is better than down" but with our tongues in so many bodies and bodies in thrall to such old maps (you say ideology, I say grammar), who can tell where the sky will fall next? Leaving us with the ever useful poetic command: register locally

I now remember Creeley grinning as he quoted

And I could not help thinking
of the wonders of the brain that
hears that music and of our
skill sometimes to record it

PEOPLE

OR NOT

Gil Ott 1951-2004

D

ear Gil,

I w
onder w

here
the dail
y

noises st
art making
poetry hap
pen hap
py

or not read
y to continue being w
hat they on
ce sounded like
the
y
were starting out to say or not being one thing being one mani
fold sound in min

d and if we believe that then here's *T*
he Brid
ge we should put a small
down payment on just
a wor
d or t
wo and the span wil

I stand i

n space

for as long

as we continue to a

id its long le

ngth or was that its stro

ng streng

th in uplif

ting our neural pathways if we

know what's go

od for us th

en we kn

ow what we kn

ow and if we do

n't then wh

at we know is so

mething else at a dis

tant altitude releasing lines

from the ch

armed stage of mel

odious incipience or not we wan

t to h

ear

the specifics of the proposed peace amid the war

of no

is

es.

Y

ours, Bob

INDIRECT ADDRESS: A GHOST STORY

[to Jacques Derrida]

I was already iterable when I woke up this A. M.:
I had begun to write to [you]

in Philadelphia and am now in New York,
dragging a motley pageant of tenses

across the first sentence
which is only just now finishing.

Before it began
the deadline for this piece

on the occasion of [your] death
had passed and of course it is even later now,

which iterates me more. Across the mirror
it must be strict and still I imagine:

no iteration. But imagining
means nothing when words

have stopped moving.
Direct address between the living

and the dead is foolish, unless
some gemütlich, unheimlich correspondence course

has already been inaugurated,
and has either of [us] signed up for that?

Here, times and places still bleed into one another,
New York, Philadelphia, yesterday, two days later,

and we continue to cut ourselves.
Courting coincidence, possibly. Myself, twice

while making dinner, nicking one thumb
(think empiricism meets formalism) and ten minutes later

grating the knuckle of the other on the cheese grater
(think pragmatism applied with brute disregard for local

circumstance). One thing bleeding into another:
can't that be one of the pleasures

of a settled art? Watercolor.
But words, think: which is more

to the point, "words bleed into one another," or
simply "words bleed"? Neither.

They're neither the neutral relays of a combinatory
enjoyment, nor the carriers

of a transcendently central
materiality of language.

"Words bleed," that's the feeling
of unstanchable vulnerability

that underlay modernism at its most Deco-baked marmoreal.
Here, where [you] have died, we remain in the midst

of a long, stuttering song
that no one now writing

can't not hear:
it's going strong, shattered into slogans

each designed
to carry the tune. Blood

and boundaries: dull old tropes
but still tripping up heels faster than ever.

O, [you] who never
seemed to like finishing a sentence

when it was always possible
to go on writing it, as if,

within what might be made intelligible,
it was always the height of noon,

now for [you] the untraceable ink
of an endless period

has put a stop to the continuous
present [you] inscribed

onto just about every word.
"I weep for Adonais, he is dead" we say

and life remains iterable.
[You're] not, however.

So questions of address
remain vexed, especially since

the language I am writing from,
flighty and false-bottomed as it is,

makes a few inflexible and awkward demands.
Here (American-English) there is no avoiding

the overlap of the sound of a formal regard
for appropriate distance—[you]—

with a more intimate noise—[you].
[You], sir, and [you], old mole,

seem to be one and the same,
at least if sounds sound like

what they're supposed to mean. Hence the brackets.
Which makes for a certain double-jointedness.

But doesn't meaning only appear
after addresses have been exchanged?

And I have addressed [you.]
[You] first appeared as a stage villain

in "Movie" in *Captive Audience*
—do I really have to tell [you] this?—

where against Grant and Hepburn [you] played
some shadowy figure with shadowy powers

suggesting an end to their regal portrayals of spontaneity.
In other words: there was a script,

or more, a counter-script, which [you] had in your possession.
At one point the poem

suggested [you] and Hepburn
had forged a certain intimacy

but it was one of those 'always already' shots,
where the audience doesn't get to see anything happening

except [your] arm handing her
a towel in the bathtub.

Next, [you] appeared in "The Marginalization of Poetry"
in propria persona, as [yourself] so to speak,

where I quoted *Glas* as an example of multi-margined writing:
"One has to understand that he

is not himself before being Medusa
to himself. . . . To be oneself is

to-be-Medusa'd . . . . Dead sure of self. . . .
Self's dead sure biting (death)" after which

I shrugged and winked:
"Whatever this might mean, and it's possibly

aggrandizingly post-feminist, man swallowing woman,"
and then issued a vague compliment:

"nevertheless in its complication of identity it
seems a step toward a more

communal and critical reading and writing
and thus useful." Useful:

that's one of those
canapes that taste of nothing

but institutional compromise.
Words are usable things

but it doesn't go the other way:
things aren't words. I can quote "Adonais"

but not the tormented street tree out front.
"Poems are made by fools like me,"

the man wrote, "but only God can quote
a tree." When [you] live by the book

[you] tote it around, die by it,
and by the book is how [you] continue.

That's the same in poetry and philosophy.
But, still, the notion of two activities forming

the basis for a critical community is,
as [you] might say, utopian.

(We might say imaginary.) Poet
and philosopher at times have issued

cordial invitations for the other
to come over and discuss the

common concerns, but there hasn't been
much pressure to actually visit.

I continued, "Glas is still, in
its treatment of the philosophical tradition,

decorous; it is marginalia, and the
master page of Hegel is still

Hegel, and Genet is Hegel too."
The names don't go away

when the eyes close. Neither do
the already crowded screens of younger readers

at least as long as the arrow of time
keeps pointing in the same direction.

And all attempts at instruction will,
somewhere along the line, find the instructors

in the discombobulated position of gesturing toward
some ideological Rube Goldberg ruin, folly, pratfall.

The poem. The concept.
But let's not let parallelism set precedents.

On the other hand, note
how the upcoming line break, although

philosophically insignificant (and semantically insignificant,
it must be said), is poetically

still up for grabs. We poets
(it must be written) really don't know,

are prohibited (structurally) from knowing
what we write before it's written, and,

in a back-eddying double-whammy,
can't really forget what's come before

the most recent word.
In that we model both the alert insouciance

of the newborn (with its millennia of entailments,
but still in-fant, un-speaking) and

the fully aged fluent inhabitant
of language flowing

around a life, offering infinite comprehension
all the way out to the sedgy banks

with fields of goldenrod beyond them
but not the algorithm that would allow for

moment by moment access to the whole story
which we never get to hold with frankly human concern

but have to address via the nerved scrimmage
of writing. Skin's mostly healed, but mind persists

in changing. Before, I'd figured [you] as some
jauntily allegorized emblem of

unknowableness and now [you] are
playing that part to perfection.

IN MEMORY

Memory lying open to the one spread naked fa
shion plate earliest front page someone signing

Memory lying open to the one spread naked fashion pl
ate blood on the wall and a little around the back door

Earliest front page a smiling man in handcuffs
staged it turns out real weapons in the trailers

Unhearable hisses Go upstairs! but me
mory's already dusted the fingerprints

Blood on the wall and a little around the back door now h
ere's a person in charge of the excitement going backstage

The pleasures of the night eyes shut maybe me
mory on the wall a little around the back door

Friendly smile but stopped by the shutter blurred
by the presses older machines heavy with capital

Upstairs the pleasures of the nigh
t smiling already "Dawn *likes* you"

Memory lying open friendly smile already dusted I'
m in the picture too at attention in front of the TV

Small bruise the picture swallowed into the
center dot and a little around the back door

Breathing in bad sectors not available
ash unreadable under the bedside light

Staged it turns out actors in charge backs
age too small bruise not a friendly spread

Rehear unrepeatable hisses b
ut memory's already upstairs

With Freud wrong and nobody right th
e picture swallowed into the center dot

Older breathing heavy with substitution
accent raconteuring so I sound like this

Real weapons get used to it with
Freud wrong and nobody right

Blood on the wall and a little around the ba
ck door holding hands like book and reader

Here we are awake tell me if it hurts
bad sectors unhearable small bruises

The picture swallowed into the cen
ter dot the only one without accent

We all say that "Dawn lik
es you" unhearable hisses

We can't be translated resurrected not that k
ind lees less brutal once you make that toast

Now here's a person in charge mayb
e excitement awake in a forged epic

But memory had son
s too another couplet

"Dawn *likes* you" sudd
en appearance of cum

Public light over everything a mess eyes shut seeking th
e pleasures of the night handcuffs backstage excitement

You can't remember them yet
stuttering in front of the epic

Trees grow leaves leaves get
educated educations fall off

The walls meet less frequently ho
lding hands like book and reader

Here we are awake earliest fro
nt page a smiling man *likes* you

Cross the bridge the one spread nak
ed when you come to it backwards

Cutting wood to fold rubles into esc
ape velocity forced awake in an epic

Chopping and sawing all day slee
p from dusk on substitute velocity

Caresses maneuvering over fix
ed scars tell me where it hurts

But memory's already dusted the fingerprin
ts escape memory lying open in the forest

Fixed stars spread throughout the day invisibl
e behind the escaping light here we are awake

Lees less brutal once you make that toas
t the pleasures of the night again tell me

71

NOTES ON MEMOIR

I can't remember when or where I bought my copy of Stendhal's *Life of Henri Brulard* but I certainly had it in 1977 in San Francisco, when I used it, along with Shackleton's *Antarctic Journals* and the letters of the Mozart family to collage "An Autobiography." Perhaps because I have such a distant relationship with my own memory, memoir in all its permutations has persistently fascinated me.

I can't remember how I found out about Stendhal—maybe Alan Bernheimer told me. It's slightly possible that after high school, college, and an MFA at Iowa I had never heard of him until Francie Shaw and I moved to San Francisco in 1976. That seems a little improbable. But I had never read him. I do remember reading *The Red and the Black* as soon as we got to San Francisco and being extremely enthused—a habit in those days. I remember sitting in Barry Watten's apartment on Connecticut St. with Barry and Bob Grenier, the three of us making a tape for Anselm Hollo. (It can hardly have been on a reel to reel tape recorder, but that's the instrument my memory seems to be providing.) Barry started off by playing a record of something that I recall as being Chinese marching music. What did Barry and Bob read into the tape? I read out a long section of *The Red and the Black;* I remember Bob saying that he thought that I, via Stendhal, was dictating a moral lesson to him. But, no, it was just that I couldn't imagine anything more interesting than those words. I can't (of course) remember the passage, except that, in the most general sense, it was a deliciously comic somber sinuous anatomization of the most passionate tragic amorous attachment.

I now remember that there was a copy of *The Red and the Black* in my parents' home in Youngstown. It must have been my mother's, possibly my sister's. I thought the title referred to a roulette wheel, flashing never knowable mixes of fate and chance throughout the casino-like spaces adults moved in, performing their adult maneuvers. It all seemed a little boring and scary. I never opened the book.

"The Freeze" in *Face Value* begins,

I remember my thighs.
It was in a movie. I was asleep,
but voting, trying to remain inconspicuous.
I saw what I saw and I felt what I felt.
At the time I thought nothing of it,

but as the policewomen started to remove her blue blouse it was my mother and I was Stendhal and the mercury was starting to wear off and I was sick, sick with desire, but also just plain sick, damaged, an exception, the only one in the non-named bourgeois world who was separated from desire. I had no job except to be witty entering salons, profound later in the evening, and rhapsodically convinced of my doubt in private, when I would throw my wig in a corner and write of the dangers of satisfaction, running with the pack in the pre-dawn

The opening line was my reaction to hearing a poem I hated that began, "I remember her thighs." Line 2 articulates, exaggeratedly, the displacement enacted in line 1. Lines 3, 4, 5 are me miming normalcy, secure in the knowledge that it's too late. The end of the long line is taken from the end of the first part of *The Red and the Black* where ___ has first consummated his affair with ___ and has to escape out the window at dawn. The husband's hunting dogs run along with the lover, silently. A pack of dogs running up should be terrifying, especially when you've just jumped out of your lover's window, but these dogs simply confirm his enacted desire. It was exhilarating and deeply surprising as I read. Does one dog lick his hands while they're running? I'll have to look it up, and the names.

Stendhal did use mercury for syphilis. Fact. How did I learn that?

Julien Sorel was his name, of course. Fact, led up to memory via mystery channels. But what was hers?

I don't want to look anything up. Fact, meaningless quixoticism.

There are sometimes minutes between paragraphs, and sometimes days. Fact.

Waves of impatience beat on conventional shores, waves of repression beat on the shores of light. Fact.

Why did Stendhal, whose real name was Henri Beyle, call his autobiography *The Life of Henri Brulard?* I remember, during one of my Stendhal effusions, discussing the spelling with Barry. How could it possibly be "dh"? he wondered. Shouldn't it at least have been "Stendahl"?

Mademoiselle de la Mole.

No, the other one. Love of his life.

My copy is a small paperback, its dimensions slightly smaller than *My Life*, though it's a bit more than twice as thick. It's pretty old, younger than me. I'm 1947; it's 1955 (dates of issue):

a VINTAGE BOOK   95¢   in Canada $1.00   K-18

The top and bottom of the front cover are bands of yellow, somewhat dirty. The middle band, from 20% down from the top to about 30% up from the bottom, is maroon. In the middle of the maroon is a white oval framing a black silhouette in profile, which I take to be of Stendhal. You can see the hair—a little bit Elvis-like, though apparently less slicked up since individual strands are visible. His nose is medium-sized, straight. His lips seem a little thin, though this is my inference from the tiny triangular white inlet that marks them. Overall, he seems stocky. He is wearing lace, vaguely visible in front of his neck and in back. The whole thing can feel rather powerful, but also, as a flat black absence of light in profile, it withholds any hint of visage, speech, motion. I've turned the book over a number of times and looked through the introductory matter to see the sentence assuring me that this is Stendhal's profile, but have never found it. Wouldn't it be great to see what Stendhal looked like? Prurient curiosity.

Of course, now I realize that this was my mother's book.

The book is broken into two halves at 174/175. My reading has done this damage. 174 starts with three asterisks, the sign of a section break, and then "A great event was in preparation for me: I was very much moved by it at the moment, but it was too late; all bonds of friendship between my father and me had been forever broken, and my horror of middle-class details and of Grenoble was henceforth invincible." The back of the paper spine adheres to the right-hand section. I'm intending to quote from 175, but this has to wait as my attention is fixed on the inside of the broken-open spine. It's a flap of beiger, rougher paper, fraying abruptly at the torn side, with a few tiny curls lifting up from it. But this vocabulary doesn't really bite into anything and I keep staring at what's not a noun, not an object, not a pattern. It's just matter, stained by time, moving back from human manufacture at its own pace. The difference between the communicative mysteries of print, lively, endless, truncated, and the brute material of the binding strikes half of me into words, leaving the rest numb. It's amazing that this was my mother's book. Who was she, to have read this in Youngstown, Ohio in the 50s with nary an interested soul around? In asking such a question I might as well be staring at the torn binding flap: no words not already my own will issue from that source.

175 starts,

of onions" was constantly in people's mouths at Grenoble.

My grandfather's only reply to his daughter's insolent reproach was to shrug his shoulders and say: "She is ill."

When I wrote "An Autobiography" I was fascinated, along with many others, by the spaces that breaking syntax and general sequence could open up. The idea was not the Burroughs' cut-up that would hex the panopticon of normative discourse, but something like Berrigan's *Clear the Range*, his white-out rewriting of a cowboy novel: "In front of him was his head," to quote from memory. One's head was somewhere in front of one: being objective and aleatory about subjectivity seemed sublimely comic.

The Life of Henri Brulard was moving and amusing in ways that were quite different from the hilarity of cut-up, collage and white-out. In some senses, the single, personal source of Brulard makes for greater distances than cut-up or random procedural work. There are intimate distances throughout the book.

At the beginning of his memoir, Stendhal-Beyle-Brulard recounts the scene where he first decides to write it. It's twilight in Rome; he stays out till dark, then heads toward a social occasion:

> I felt harassed. I was wearing a pair of white trousers of English stuff; and I wrote inside, on the band: "16 October 1832, I am going to be fifty," contracted like this, so that it should not be understood: Imgo ingt obef if ty.

Both language and the places of memory are bizarrely present and ineffable. Always there are at least three times, past, present, and future. Here is the death, in 1796, of a mean aunt, possibly his father's mistress:

> One winter evening, as it seems to me, I was in the kitchen, about seven o'clock, at the point H, opposite Marion's cupboard. Someone came and said: "She has passed away." I threw myself on my knees at the point H to thank God for this great deliverance.
>
> If Parisians are as foolish in 1880 as they are in 1835, this way of taking the death of my mother's sister will cause me to be looked upon as barbarous, cruel, and abominable.

The sincere and histrionic are so often mixed in Stendhal. But there's also "point H," an icon of the place itself, where his knees (not then, but now articulate) actually touched down. His deliverance was into the ineffable legibility of memoir, no one's memory, no one's perception, endless excluded middles where desire desires its ideal negative space. Torn beige paper. Quoting Stendhal again:

```
      a    d       i   l   ine    pg     de    r
V. A . A . M. M. A. A    . A    . M    . C. G. A .
1         2       3       4 5   6
```
(Mme Azur, whose Christian name I have forgotten)

The bodies of lovers, numbered, devolve to letters in the dust.

Stendhal is disgusted when mathematicians can't agree about infinity. One says that parallel lines will never meet at infinity. But "that egregious animal Louis Monge" says they will meet. Stendhal asks M. Chabet for an explanation: "'My child,' he said, putting on that paternal manner which is so ill-sited to the foxes of Dauphinéthe manner of Édouard Mounier [a peer of France, in 1836]—'my child, you will know later.'"

It's now "later," children.

It o oam f if ty (t w o).

Pa ra   ll e ll   ine sd o   not me   et.

THE DREAM OF THE BED

Mark Perelman 1909-2003

It was so long ago I barely remember,
and when I remember I barely believe.
And the propositions of belief
have nothing to do with the senses,
my thin companions through all this. Thus
if the vision is silent, we remain in the dark.

It was last week. I had been asleep
the better part of a year, throughout
the century, looking back it was solid dream.

In the dream there were different cities
to fly between, and in the cities
solid floors to uphold me,
walls and ceilings to act as shields,
doors standing for choice and acceptance.
What vision saw, I saw.
What hearing heard, I as well heard,
and I touched what touch touched.
It was that simple a sum.

I had watched throughout the week
but what I watched
and what I was watching for
tongue is not permitted,
nor fingers, nor ears,
none of our nimblenesses may play there.

One becomes a digit inside a thimble.
When I awoke it was there: a bed.
A bed in a dream.

I looked. It looked as if it could
teach the old head a last thing,
as if breath could pause there
till the balances regained their poise.

Covered in chrome,
it shone with generations of improvements.
Up was thoughtfully provided for, rolling over
could be accomplished without danger.
It could minister as its controls dictated.
Anyone could be the you addressed, the you held.

The address was sober, as full of comfort
as could be arranged, but the addressee
had sprung a perfect leak.
The lake had spread everywhere
and nothing could rise above its low surface.

What could such a bed say?
Its chrome rails shone, its soft platform
continued to uphold the absenting cause of its being there.

Just a few noises.
Repeated gurgles, this is the way.
Stop. This is the way.
Stop. Just a bit deeper.

Vision flew to the window. Glass.
Hearing reached the sea. Caught
in those folds. Touch the old colors,
the wishes achieved long ago.
Flags too tired to address the air,
no longer distinguishable.

Change keys, take the watch, change
the sheets, wash them, burn them
in the sun. Put the feet
in a bag, and the ancient deeds,
put the head in some one-sided
approximation of rest.

When the cause it served was fully gone, the bed was wheeled out.

Fly home alone. But that was to be the future,
which is to be the present,
which is what the vision grants.

TODAY'S LAMENT

for Emily Steiner

You'd think a thousand years of laments would be enough,
but no. Now I have to write one.

First, it seems, you get stuck in these systems,
then you have to explain yourself to them.

I now think my kinsmen had secret plans behind those more or less smiling faces.
Reason is fretted with anger since it's been forced to live here under an oak tree
   in a suburban cave.
The streets are gloomy, overgrown with cars,
lit and crosslit by the varnished light of debt.
The cars move or not in their sullen variousness. Some shine, some do not.

You'd think it would be possible
to make macaroni and cheese without having to get in the car,

but no.
No cheese: no macaroni and cheese.

Aren't a thousand years of laments enough?
Apparently not.

There's a little parmesan, but no cheddar.
There's a problem with the globe,
but no view.
So it's out on the tossing waves to Superfresh.

Fresh tears, fresh words drawn from my own sorrowful lot.
I can say that.
"Weigh your 'sharp cheddar cheese.'
Move your 'sharp cheddar cheese' to the belt."

In this wide second, I am seized with longings.

"Weigh your 'broccoli rabe.'
Move your 'broccoli rabe' to the belt."

I have not suffered such hardships as now.
"Weigh their 'pretending, plotting, murderous, smiling faces.'
Move their 'pretending, plotting, murderous, smiling faces' to the belt."
This is not a generic thousand-year-old lament, but fresh today.

I would now explain the lit and crosslit gloom of the system
that makes us live most wretchedly, far from one another,
but no.

Explain to my friendless kinsmen, tossed
with fresh gloomy longings, vigilant to the generic clutch of anguish,
explain to the Superfresh stronghold.

"Weigh your 'thousand years of linguistic change.'
Move your 'thousand years of linguistic change' to the belt."

You'd think one car would be enough,
one long world
out from this cave under these tossing systematic dawns.
You'd think, after a thousand years,

but no.
I draw these words from my endless list seized with crosslit longings.

"Weigh
your 'endless list seized with crosslit longings.'
Move
your 'endless list seized with crosslit longings'
to the belt."

A thousand years, crossed off, crouching under the parking lot,
my lot.

                            [after the Old English "Wife's Lament"]

A GUIDE TO *HOMAGE TO SEXTUS PROPERTIUS*

I

Now if ever it is time to translate modernism into a contemporary idiom
into "something to read in normal circumstances"
to quote *Homage to Sextus Propertius*, one of the few moments when Pound's poetry
was fully contemporary, when he felt the distentions of writing time most generously
and thus most accurately.

II

In *Propertius* Pound was able to write as though
the present had a past and that past had a future
which wasn't just a reproduction of the original present
because he was changing it with the very words of the poem
finally breathing the actual air of modernity
first sniffed in Baudelaire, temporary-and-eternal modernity.

So the equations that scored social space into such exacting drawing rooms
could open out into a workable surface
on which writing could move.

It looked like there might be room for more than one generation
a bit of an age-playground for noise, talk
something better than soundtrack music
            —for once Pound escaped
from that timeless tone or at least had managed some time off.

There was room for women and men.

For once Pound turned his back on heroism
and made women (though he calls them girls) the primary audience.
In the words of a scolding Apollo:
        "Who has ordered a book about heroes?

"You need, Propertius, not think

"About acquiring that sort of reputation.

"Soft fields must be worn by small wheels,

"Your pamphlets will be thrown, thrown often into a chair

"Where a girl waits alone for her lover."

III

1917, who needs a book about heroes?

Chronology is always a sore spot with Pound.
Propertius is dated 1917 in *Personae* but it sounds like 1915,
with Gaudier still invincibly alive in the trenches,
thus allowing our poet to greet the war with an elegant stage-yawn:

Out-weariers of Apollo will, as we know, continue their Martian generalities.

Pound then shows said generalities rolling out their blood red carpets
to receive the tread of imperial distention:

Tigris and Euphrates shall, from now on, flow at Caesar's bidding,
Tibet shall be full of Roman policemen.

The snappy insouciance of that couplet is part of the best of Pound's legacy. In the
first line he simultaneously sounds and skewers the tedious formalism of the syco-
phantic-prophetic where the poet affirms the divinely-sanctioned god-like power
of the state: "Tigris and Euphrates shall, from now on, flow at Caesar's bidding"; he
then quickly untunes this in the next line via mismatches in diction, history and
geography which are puzzlingly instructive as they lighten up the ear: "Policemen"
an anachronism and an Americanism; "Tibet" utterly unrelated to the Roman
empire. But beyond simple incongruity Pound is constructing a witty equation.
Propertius had been sarcastically assenting to Augustus's world-rule: there would
be Roman legions in the utterly far-away provinces, Parthia or Britain. Thus, in
Pound's time-travel, contemporary London gets to hear itself described as "Tibet,"
the exotic end of all known things. Though the message of the couplet is ultimate-
ly tame—empire rules the world—its wit displays itself as the fastest thing around.

And today Pound's prophetic bridge between past and present still stands: Iraq is full of American soldiers.

IV

Write in two times, two languages
neither of them simply new or simply old.
Think, tongue, notebook open by the warm bed.
Hold hands, Pennsylvanian, under the table, Bride Scratton's hand, say
explore the logomelopoesis of sticking close to women.
You hadn't done it much before and you hardly—if ever—did it again.
For once you heeded Oppen's later warning: "Only one mistake, Ezra!
You should have talked to women."

Imagine a world without Homer, Pound, without Virgil (without Mussolini):

> And my ventricules do not palpitate to Caesarial *ore rotundos,*
> Nor to the tune of the Phrygian fathers.

> And in the mean time my songs will travel,
> And the devirginated young ladies will enjoy them
> > when they have got over the strangeness.

V

You yourself were now devirginated
and via the classics you could write about sex
in your own present, a book-filled one to be sure,
but free of troubadorian uplift:

Stele

After years of continence
   he hurled himself into a sea of six women.
Now, quenched as the brand of Meleagar,
   he lies by the poluphloisboious sea-coast."

VI

Propertius compliments itself on being soft, on its sexy slither:

    you ask on what account I write so many love-lyrics
    And whence this soft book comes into my mouth.
    Neither Calliope nor Apollo sung these things into my ear,
      My genius is no more than a girl.

      . . . . if hair is mussed on her forehead,
    If she goes in a gleam of Cos, in a slither of dyed stuff,
    There is a volume in the matter . . . .
      And if she plays with me with her shirt off,
      We shall construct many Iliads. . . .
      We shall spin long yarns out of nothing.
    Thus much the fates have allotted me.

Here Pound and so-called Cynthia are their own fates,
spinning their own thread of days.
And the Empire can mind its own business:

      if, Maecenas,
    I were able to lead heroes into armour, I would not,
    Neither would I warble of Titans, nor of Ossa spiked onto Olympus. . . .
    Nor of Thebes in its ancient respectability.

VII

Chronology was always a sore spot. At more or less the same time as this step away from them—nobody had written like this in English in 1916—Pound was positing his more usual audience of Serious Men, timeless, ultra-moderne. He has, he thinks, rejected the soft book, emphatically spitting it out, inserting instead a hard pacifier manufactured, he informs us, in 19th-century French fiction: "If a man has not in the year of grace 1915 or 1916 arrived at the point of enlightenment carefully marked by the brothers De Goncourt in A.D. 1863, one is not admitted to the acquaintance of anyone worth knowing. I do not say that a person holding a different view would be physically kicked downstairs if he produced a different opinion in an intelligent company; our manners have softened; he would be excreted in some more spiritual manner."

Pound is rarely as unintentionally funny as he is here. But such sentences do admit to their author having a body, acknowledging that excreting is a process engaged in even by those "worth knowing."

Twenty-seven years later, in the cage, Pound will write, "I heard it in the s.h.   a suitable place / to hear that the war was over." But in between those two moments he's spurned Joyce's excretory inclusiveness and had tried to purify the world. The Hell Cantos are a prime example, and the longing to celebrate the "clean slayne" in Canto XXX. But back now to Pound's 1916 prose and our wounded chronology, since it is now time for Pound to enunciate the lesson:

"In December 1876, Edmond de Goncourt wrote the following sentences: 'You cannot ask us at this time of day to amuse the young lady in the rail-road carriage. I think we have acquired, since the beginning of the century, the right to write for formed men, without the depressing necessity of fleeing to foreign presses.'"

Pound comments on how obvious this is: "There you have it."

But the commentator himself is not so obvious: "We were most of us unborn, or at the least mewling and puking, when those perfectly plain, simple, and one would have supposed obvious sentences were put together."

Pacifier in mouth, Pound miming dignified elegance.

VIII

With *Propertius* the displacements were more conscious and reached farther out
and you were getting a little closer to home.

The Empire was ankle-deep in fresh-flowing blood, the top salons
weren't absolutely closed, and you had discovered
that it was possible to write about women
(plural and with a small w) in the same language that could also encompass
arma virumque.

       In one breath
you could point with disdain at the wars along the distended
assumptions of empire and without having to inhale

you could move over the articulate smoothness
of a body that very much

wasn't yours. Then it would be time
to take another breath.

IX

It's hard to breathe well when there are gods around
floating in the azure air, bright gods and Tuscan,
recumbent on Miltonic adjective postpositional,
back before dew was shed.

In that dry Mediterranean climate
the gods have no homework

they wear, when they choose
loose-fitting attractive clothes

there are no references to look up
no conference papers to write

only the pleasant present
good on the skin
seemingly unlimited supplies
of excellent hors d'oeuvres and fresh gossip

but the gods turn out to be
hard acts to book.
They'll appear (briefly) in big set pieces
costing an arm and a leg
(Canto II—can't afford to do *that* too many times!)

but to get the gods to actually impart some information
there's about as much hope of that
as of cashing a check written on water
A Draft of XXX Cantos
a thousand and one cantos
whatever the going rate, you acted like you could pay it
rushing forward to pick up the bill each time
stuffing them in your pocket
because, anyway, the gods were going to pay.

But the gods don't pick up checks
they display perfection
from the source, easy to drink from

but difficult to find. Impossible really, unless one of them shows you.
And the question is: Can the route be taught?

Taught in a poem? taught
to many, or to only a few?

or is it that no one can simply *learn*
how to gain access? Pound, you learned things and

you taught. But can that which you teach
be detached from your own practice of teaching?

Or is "teach" no more than an intransitive, godlike verb?
the sound of judgment echoing and re-echoing

over everything that is new
upon which dew
simply must not fall?

Perhaps that was what you heard the gods teaching
as you walked "sheer into 'nonsense'"

and saw "two eyes like the eyes of a wood-creature"
peering at you "over a brown tube of wood."

But if anything can neutralize the new it's the gods.
So that your predicted history grew monstrously encumbered

and never arrived in any form you could ever get your benighted listeners to
    recognize.

X

Will *The Cantos* outlast the Pound industry?
Or have they made it so that any poetry, to be read outside its group
must manufacture its own industry?

Do the scholiasts' clarifications
do more than add to the rubbish at the base camps?

Heat-soured milk
overburdened verbal habits
the cold peak beckoning.

Nevertheless, Pound,
it is not with your demi-gods I would walk

nor would I suggest others sign up for that endless afternoon hike
neath sun-beat tho it be.

I won't make a pact with you
just as you didn't make one with Propertius

not that I'm unmindful of what you did there
staging a new kind of battle of the Moderns vs. the Ancients
playing on both sides of the net, frigidaire patent in one hand
while issuing party invitations in translationese with the other

"Though my house is not propped up by Taenarian columns from Laconia
(associated with Neptune and Cerberus)"
— that is *not* something someone "in the throes of some particular emotion"
would actually *say*. It's something you

wrote. For pleasure

in flimsy exception
to general war.

WRONG COUNTRY

for William Carlos Williams

Yours were the first names I saw
a self-conscious speaking tube in love
with the loud gaps
into which we'd plunge, my idea

of you and the other action figures
attached to the air currents
lifting the words that move together
or not at all

I read you?
A you? Now
divided by then
to amuse the ones to come

You'd hate the web
the buyable things against the screen
even more you'd hate
liking things like that

Quatrains helped or were you
against yourself on principle?
Meanings are still at large
The wills of so many involved

Cherry pink bra strap
lost to thought
and that person's dictionary of response
exciting the senses

to open a new document
A full day beneath the jets
hardly a shred of local left
America's sinking, everyone sees

VOICE PLAY

ONLY ONE OF US IS HENRY JAMES:

The thing reigned supreme but was evanescent. Arms in unconscious contact with mahogany-stained pine were junior partners to the keystrokes that aimed to put the mind in trust of this happily made thing the recurrent dream of justice feeling actual stuff from outside tuned into one mode by sheer plod of getting written deeper into its own current superfluity than any reading could peer without finally admitting the glitter of any particular was for all intents and purposes bottomless and finding in time that any word skein thrown no matter how directly downwind might as well have been an airline pension plan tattooed on a choppy square mile of the North Atlantic for all the further we'd journeyed toward the thing we'd come to think was simply there, ours for the making. One clutch of fingers wiped an unlaundered handkerchief across a forehead while another lay low to allow brain or we should say eyes to read another sentence a little differently for the key-strokes to then lug a bit further toward a future of the most intensely general interest.

The sheltering page of capital cast its vertical shadow across all things met with in the life splayed in the new century into shatter of reflected time the vision of the achieved whole thing left to the teams riding their mounts directly toward the low stiles jumping difference from the standard phrasing which kept lowing from nextdoor pastures less and less plausibly each season it must be said.

Nothing for you in those noises is an incommensurate nothing for me here in full justification or the plain one-paragraph novel (insert food scene here) smacking lips and pursing them at the sight of mutual wounds reflected in sibilant readers. Which also means touching knees under the table.

For decades it was thought these were the cure. Then gradually people began to realize that they were thinking and touching different things. Even under the same covers.

IDEAL READER:

What you write is perfectly true.
It makes me want to think so too.

STUDENT PUBLICATION:

Yes, sir, I was fucking ablativeabsolutely looking out the window—
Someone has to translate the sacred language of the clouds.

POUND'S PENIS (aside)

Bathed morning and evening
in the filthiest newsprint,
you're surprised they call
my spontaneous history "cold"?

Roughnecks hv/ recd/ insffnt/ attn/

Phallic & ambrosial,
we fought for the flag of European jungle excitement.
Only a cad
wd/ look up meaning.

Roughnecks hv/ recd/ insffnt/ attn/

Long ghosts ago, to tease me,
Gaudier died.
I remain alone, sticking out.

Roughnecks hv/ recd/ insffnt/ attn/

EPIC PROPORTIONS:

Alexandria Florence Paris San Francisco
Youngstown Brattleboro Traverse City Rochester
the past charming itself
claims every trireme every oar every stroke every charming
bead of sweat
dropped on deck

The naked forms of force
telnetting into the single skull
beneath the waves of whispered transmission
Stroke! Stroke!

THEATER OF CRUELTY:

Wouldn't you like to know

HUSBANDS AT THEIR DESKS:

Isn't it a bit late to be hating the *Four Quartets?* They don't hate you; they only hate themselves and that lightly with intimate self-regard as they twirl their well-typed verbal lassos any prey having by prior agreement escaped. It stands in a dream of formally pure sound ears cocked eyes impossible to engage.

T. S. Eliot did correspond with Groucho Marx real name Julius, hobby: reading, favorite book: *The Trial.*

POETIC SEX:

No rush, take as long as you want.
When you're finished
those moans go back
in the Surrealist portfolio

I'm sorry: it can't leave the room.
The list?
Not a problem. Take one with you.

ENEMY READER:

As soon as the initial line
hoves over the horizon
the first thing that comes to mind
is everything else.

The captain goes down with the poem
but that doesn't mean
I have to keep reading.

Which reminds me.
I hear your autobiography's
been remaindered.

HOW MUCH IS THAT POET IN THE WINDOW?

Ink's overflowing as I sit and read, brokenhearted,
observing the print, the manner,
the time. The rebellious czars
are trashing the money, making lines
infinitely cheap.

FAITH BASED LYRIC

I'm bored.
A few more seconds like this
and there won't be a safe place in my mind

Salute till it bleeds
the first time for love
after that for need

I've been bored for all my life
History is the same old shit on the tracks
that weren't that fascinating the first time around

So professor
tell that to your class mired in individual collectivity
Better bring a shovel

THE JACK SPICER MEMORIAL NEURON

Here's your new meter, Pilgrim.
If it's itchy you know what to do.

STEIN AND MISS MURPHY

There's something especially lovely about any one wet flexible square inch
next to other equally lovely square inches
lit by love-light

connected by nothing but transforming bliss
where legs meet eyes and the sky is just where the sound always said it would be
the century come true this time

it's good that you can see how things are
that you can lift things up and see nothing is secret any more

ENVOI

Drink this.

It's on the house.
It's our house now.
That's what it says in the script you paid us with

It wasn't enough to learn to read it.
But we learned anyway.
You taught us
to read with our backs.
Our backs to you, that is.
And now we know that you can't read our mouths or tell what's in our eyes.
So we can't exactly say
we weren't paid.

That great opening line?
Tongue through the door?
My pay stub.

NONSONNETS

VEILED PORTRAIT

It's a big
hard to find place
to go for a shorter than
short time

       The corner store
it's not

     It's a hard
to hide place to be for
ever and a day

        Whichever you want say it
however you think it should be said
                  Still

it will stay
more or less the same
kind of a shame like
the old days but better
ones ahead a bit
of an opening it
sometimes looks like

          For now
we go there as ourselves
us and it.

IDENTITY MY TOMB

The past was past
but like the past
it now starts to remain
in plain ideological sight
stretched & v. fertile
golden autumn harvest stuff
bristling with RSVPs

We were born there
and however the social tune
breaks it will frame
the old punchline
when we leave

Who wouldn't want
to change at least
some pages
even if these words
must stay to show
what couldn't be
seen there?

—found on the flyleaf of *Late Marxism* July 29, 2002

NUT CASE

I can almost taste
the almond paste
around the past

Sweetest part's
the silent e
letting that a be
long on the tongue

First things first
and last things last
long longing
before is can be

In between
I screen
to see
what means

What meant
is the stick
always bends

in water
to touch bottom
or better

to find a place
to rendezvous
with you

POSTCARD POETICS

Without everything, nothing.
Beyond everything, nothing.

Well, maybe something either way,
one thing at a time.

Everything
is there,

hiding in some
present or other.

Address is crucial. Remember
when we

almost become an item?
Instead: a memoir, and a

little dirt, if you
care to dig. Something,

I suppose. Better than nothing?
It depends how

you read. And if.
Everything, almost.

Oh, yes: circulation.
23¢ on July 1st.

Some recent year,
one with an exact number

History's not funny,
but don't shoot me, either.

POE AND MIRROR

Hi, like
a top-hatted
rabbit, I'm
the time
it takes
to shape
what comes
next, leaving
some out
for reflection

It's only one
self cudgeling letters
to cajole affection
for words' heirs,
human and inhumane
dents and duchesses,
Jack, Jill, and
you, too, Spot
and Cog, so
keep polishing those
crowns or abdicate!

MY POUND DECODER RING

Le Paradis n'est pas artificiel
                              but is jagged,
For a flash,
              for an hour,
Then agony,
              then an hour,
                            then agony,
Hilary stumbles, but the Divine Mind is abundant
                    unceasing
                    improvisatore
Omniformis
          unstill
and that the lice turned from the manifest;
              overlooking the detail
and their filth now observes mere dynamic;
That the Pontifex ceased to be holy
    — that was in Caesar's time—
          who was buggar'd
and the coin ceased to be holy,
        and, of course,
                        they worshiped the emperor.

[C 92, 640]

Poetry isn't an art facial,

                    but is jagged,

flushes,

        stays hot,

then crumples,

        stays hot,

                then crumples,

agèd jokes, but the Reading Horizon is agile

        undulating

        not what you thought

over the top

        unrepeatable

so that: the meter readers turned to their manuals,

        cementing the detachments

and the institutes now dish up mere panorama;

so that: the Present ceased to be legible

      —that was in the Stein Era—

        who had great sex

and new sense started making sense,

      but, of course,

             they re-ordered the anthologies.

PENSIVE ALLEGRO

Not me, that's
cold as light
is fast
and we eye-
ing the immensely
gone past
tumble down behind
things that pull hard
until we hear
nothing but those
particular spills.

It's your lucky day
first half
of no time
empty-headed
hearing putting
things on hold
running as far
as there are selves
to call the tune
leading edges
to touch
because that's
who we are.

JUST THIS ONCE

for Tom Raworth

a page solid card stock nothing further known yet the line has come to an end

finger slides down known contour press lift a slight swerve 5:40 muggy walls
  still yellow

a kind of accomplishment it ends up feeling pretty good

the golden meatball free downloads as far as the mind can see

stop! my reading eye never dragged me beyond this line

the next at most it hurts inside my shoulder blades back to where I don't want
  to know

body continuing its drill

achy sweet tooth tied to the tracks

solid cardstock for tonight's denouement addressing the desiring class that
  means you

denounce the insidious perpetration and creation of idiots idiot!

known moves no one move

right angles thus reason is not totally plucked from the senses but by now the
  logic bill is huge

bush busk buck fuck not all words are the same some directions work
  some do not

feeling around before the first layer of light in the sky

heart rhythms in some sort of counting contest with the sources

one? right? agreed?

real size until further notice 12:39 get back to me

MIND, GRAMMAR AND THE ETHICS OF NOMINALISM

The mind is itself
by repetitious fiat
nobly doing the dishes
by the burnt out light
of oddly costumed centuries

Flatter than any page
grammar illuminates
the celebrated longing
parts of speech
have for one another

Happy the physical
specimen that dares
name itself and whose
respect for the means at hand is
like them, finite.

ROME

To think in sentences leads to a trashy middle ground just like this.

They begin, they aim to get to the middle, for all the good that does,
and they end, for this relief much thanks.

No one has seen exactly how they get to the past. Reading always masks that.
But it also makes it happen, and they get there and start adding up.

We agree about calling it the past even if we don't agree about calling each
other we except in private spaces.

I know I don't and I'm not alone.

But I used to. We all did.
We were small, our overactive oceans structually thwarted
but ready to get up and hurl another wave at the shore.

It was a soiled love
but love for all that.

Not every transaction goes through
tangled deja vus and I've-never-been-here-befores jostle for place in line.

Why call it "Rome"?
What's it going to be? Question? Narrative? Yielding courtesy?
The Eternal City or a kind of stately eructation based on fluctuating
    property values?

Just lay it out and leave it.

To think in sentences leads to novel specimens of desire.
"If you love it so much why don't you marry it?" and so on.

Finally: a proposal.

THE JOB

I'm in the appetite business
outside jobs mostly
and then the subjective ones
try getting paid for those

You know how when I get home
I'm listless, poking food
museum Saturdays membership drives
whistles done screaming and dreams long since come true
a sort of Mommy-kissing-Santa-Claus silence under the vitrines

I'm the same differential persistence as you
which I want access to
want for want to vanquish want
like breathing in some logical sequence

Touch mine to yours and vice versa
that'll be nice

UNTITLED SAYS IT ALL

The lens gathers to a locus solus
and I want to crack the glittering book wide open

That's a couple
to a wet thought

naked
in shame's shrine

all the light
staying under the lamp

Variatease
the life of spied enchantment

TEA TIME

Make the tea with the petals
Keep your eyes open
Let me see them
drinking things in

Pull back the covers
to our days
in the right order
this one on top

License the tea
we like to drink
Dilated details
called down to the shade

The mood's more
attractive than gravity
consciously unconscious
both ways admit it

TACTICS

To write I
nibble thoughtfully
on any named
part of you
is to abandon
any claim

on the National
Book Critics Circle
award for
this or any
other year

Still, a rose
by its frank namelessness
is a general claim
on what passes
for tongue and word
touching, a
slacker's paradise

HABITS OF THE ANCIENTS

When I held you in my arms
we fell
        from habit
like living rock
around a long-lived sun

When you hold me in your head
I come from habit
        back from the hall
where the ancestors stand
tense in a tableau vivant
poised to enter the present into the record
                              the record
                                    the necropolitan record

ANOTHER

I think I used to
have one, it was
kind of like this
one but not quite,
different, a little
rounder on top,
smooth and shiny,
with a dip, a place
I used to push down,
it was very much
like this one, more
curved, not quite
as dark, though I
might be wrong,
in fact I think this
is the one I'm sure

THE TASK OF THE TRANSLATOR

This got meant onto a page
inside a set of moments
one evening of a day
which will never die
now that it is night
       poeticians sung to sleep long since
       feet to the famous flames

And once meant it leapt kicking
against the prick inside

Again, it's saying, write me again! Now!

which makes me know
this once while I forget for good
       that each knows nothing better than anyone else
       that my nothing is the same as everyone's
       that to write touches down faster
than any word falls, ethical statistician
onto its sword of many colors
dyeing the second sea black & white

       and that once in the twist
of the lines there's nothing
but to watch the
wet waves dry
and let the client walk.

FUBAR

TANK TOP

The remote isn't that big a deal

But I'm asking. Do you have the remote? It was right here

Are you sitting on it? Check

Look under the corpse. That's where it usually is

You just don't want to get up

I don't need to get up. I'd feel it

Your butt isn't that sensitive

My butt is as sensitive as it needs to be

You are becoming a serious corpse potato

I'd feel it

I would love to see what else is on

It's under the corpse

Pathetic. We both want to see what else is on. This is terrible

But "terrible" doesn't automatically mean I'm going to want to see the thing you
  think is unterrible

Isn't that another reason for you to look?

It's another reason for you. In fact, why don't you do it for no reason?

Just get up and change it then. Are you too paralyzed without the remote to get
up and look for the remote?

No, the thing about things is that they are things, if not always just the thing
But a person, perhaps playing with a thingee perhaps not it doesn't matter
even if one has a thing about certainty
can appreciate the mutability of the whole thing
It's a good thing and therefore
STOP THIS

CURRENT POETICS

Going into Iraqi refugees was the last thing on most investors' minds
but suddenly that was where all the money had gone
First thing anybody knew the sun had really set, gone down for good

It has the unbearable presence of a bad dream
a monster telethon where the mute isn't working
except you can feel pain too

Bad preaching and worse theology
with porn the only commodity still behaving itself
a marriage everyone should have seen coming

While somewhere in the extreme back yard
the fastest most expensive machines are rattling the cage of the enemy nation
   state de jour
even as your own is being rattled

There's a noble symmetry in human endeavor. Two hands, two eyes,
   mobile mouth
All that's desirable desiring

But this other spectacle is not for viewing

the secret fraternity torture with all the details in denial
but apparently shot on site

That's the current poetics
You can't imitate it and it doesn't have a plot
It's where they bury people and where people are born
— very young, as Zukofsky says and he would have known

dream narrative with the usual neocon displacements
how the head pronoun was forced
to gather shrieks of enemy combatants in a golden cup

THE REMOTE

Lord's willing only to obeyers
roped in a circle
parents watch the scantest detail
humane hate
based on group gods

Heaven understands the catalogue of the methods
Shock as burning good
with a hot Messenger
irons dripping acid Its will the skin is where it alights
torture prayer of that private Iraq

And with the new
elected of course
cutting out tongues
for personal rape strength

THREE COINS IN A FOUNTAIN

You may understand the meanings
but these words
are beyond anyone's control

The words are all good
it's the meanings that
are mostly not

Troops part of holiday scene
as primal anxiety parts waves
paints them red

Swimming into speech
with characteristic splashes
but leaving something to be desired

Please return to your sets
we are encountering
nation states rending flesh

A second trip
to the store and still
the bank is muddy

Placard scrawled with old headlines
hung around the neck
of the dying outsider

Reception's the only religious concept left
the terminator's face personal at last
corrections page 2 next day

It's easy to save things
on a computer
anywhere else is a problem

Pixilated centerpieces
with our enraged siblings
we have lost the social portion of our meaning

Force at a distance
annihilating all that's known
to a Diebold vote in our Green Zones

SUNDAY MORNING

Complacencies of the money shot
as she or he, whichever is wanted
robe loose, lazily rubs the poor box
while the decor stands as still as
the forest primevil in medium focus.

The viewer turns around in a controlled mental circle
like a dog getting ready to lie down
but more advanced, thanks to evolution
and the intelligent design of the couch

FINISH THIS

the empty store

glimpses of bruised, twisted, torn out

Get organized or is just plain "is" the only verb allowed anymore?

If I "am"
then you "are"
Or we could compromise
We "might be"
"if all goes well"

HOST

I make my signature gesture of including you
by underlining my solitary position
here in the center. How are you
—not all of you—just you, there
in the yellow? What's your name?

Rosemary? *Water?* Walter. I'm sorry.
Not that your name is Walter.
It's a perfectly good name. I
wouldn't say great. Walter
Cronkite: now that's not bad.
News is literature that stays
news. Not bad. Applause.

Walter, you say you open books
to *find out what is going on?*
And then to *escape it?* Don't
we all? Now here's a good, bookish question:
Is the world is natural?
Rosemary? *Evangeline?* I guess it's
going to be a long night. Whatever
your name is, you have no idea?
You're not either I bet.
Natural. Laughter.
Hand me another question will you, Ed?
And I know it's Ed.
Laughter. They're not laughing at you they're
laughing with you, Ed.

Okay, here's one.
Why aren't there any women torturers?

Because there aren't any women.

Oh, there are now?
Who writes these anyway?
Then why aren't there any men torturers?
I give up. Because there aren't any
men? Laughter. Sorry, Walter
I forgot about you.

MOSUL

There's really nothing on.
A conveyer belt with packages on it

This particular lunch is free
but you better watch your mouth

The master serves a free lunch without sequence or consequence
all you can eat it's edible
there's ice water medics available

And after lunch there are a certain number of hospital beds
but there's nothing on
Instant replay's useless

Our master is an angry god
behind the face very angry
someone must have done something very wrong

Bodies given over to orgies of obedience
how much gas in the tank an enraging question

And the entire city watches the operation before the Super Bowl
Republicans completely tender toward biology, patience for all the details
the screw holding the bones together while the ligaments learn to knit

The operations out of Mosul are virtuoso
tedious avant-garde tasks
reconnecting senses reactions abilities to read gestures make decisions pull triggers
all shredded into fried rice

That's for the avant-garde medics to deal with
Let the experts publish their articles about them in their itty-bitty journals

Fried *rice*, just a metaphor for a mashed up body
social ribbons of information as delicate as yours, tattered and ripped

He went "into this period"
"praying for strength to do the
Lord's will," praying that he be
"As good a messenger of His
will as possible," adding that
He prays also "for personal
strength," And not forgetting,
finally, to ask "for Forgiveness."

BEATING THE BUSHES

Evolution started in the 19th century
No real reason
And stopped in the 21st
No real reason

So now we have to keep going back
and defend the past
which has become such a dump

Grab your bananas, men,
and squeeze!

Bang on your chests
when you hear the beat!

He's playing good shepherd
on the pig farm again

Why do nameless trees
under the mindless sky

of the precognitive president
have to take up the slack?

Of what? Why does now
have to be History's

nap time the ferocious
sleepers saying anything

to keep control of the monetary public
so they can hunt in private

To the faces beyond the screen
he makes the secret sign

to eat what's there
as it disappears into some unseen account

trading good views
for shows of force

racheted up
by the eternal boredom

of the entertained, fleeing
the future, sulking in the reruns

And if you can identify with that
then you're already to Expert level

where your only nemesis
is random storage

and your modus operandi
is a news story

denied, one detail at a time, many days on each detail
weeks sucked down

minutes sorted by Up Yours
into episodes of Gotcha

as told to Fuck You
a presentation of You Already Swallowed

And so
clothes on

or off
the cliff or on

live or tape
delay

life delay or
now, never, missed the boat

or tossed on the high pitched seas of megalopolan systematic chance

what's to lose
by telling power
to leave its names outside?

This is when
the doors are open
Offer good today only

No loopholes, nothing
you wouldn't want
to be in the same room with

The chief forensic pathologist told me Jamadi was alive and well when he walked
in. The SEALs were accused of causing head injuries before he arrived, but he had
no significant head injuries—certainly no brain injuries that would have caused
death

He had injuries to his ribs. You don't die from broken ribs. But if he had been hung
up and had broken ribs, that's different

Asphyxia is what he died from—as in a crucifixion

The plastic bag could have impaired his breath, but he couldn't have died from that alone

If his hands were pulled up five feet—that's to his neck. That's pretty tough. That would put a lot of tension on his rib muscles, which are needed for breathing. It's not only painful—The muscles tire, the breathing function is impaired, so there's less oxygen entering the bloodstream

The hood would likely have compounded the problem, because the interrogators can't see his face if he's turning blue. We see a lot about a patient's condition by looking at his face. By putting that goddam hood on, they can't see if he's conscious. It also doesn't permit them to know when he died

ROOF BOOKS

- Andrews, Bruce. **Co**. Collaborations with Barbara Cole, Jesse Freeman, Jessica Grim, Yedda Morrison, Kim Rosefield. 104p. $12.95.
- Andrews, Bruce. **Ex Why Zee**. 112p. $10.95.
- Andrews, Bruce. **Getting Ready To Have Been Frightened**. 116p. $7.50.
- Benson, Steve. **Blue Book**. Copub. with The Figures. 250p. $12.50
- Bernstein, Charles. **Controlling Interests**. 80p. $11.95.
- Bernstein, Charles. **Islets/Irritations**. 112p. $9.95.
- Bernstein, Charles (editor). **The Politics of Poetic Form**. 246p. $12.95; cloth $21.95.
- Brossard, Nicole. **Picture Theory**. 188p. $11.95.
- Cadiot, Olivier. **Former, Future, Fugitive**. Translated by Cole Swensen. 166p. $13.95.
- Champion, Miles. **Three Bell Zero**. 72p. $10.95.
- Child, Abigail. **Scatter Matrix**. 79p. $9.95.
- Davies, Alan. **Active 24 Hours**. 100p. $5.
- Davies, Alan. **Signage**. 184p. $11.
- Davies, Alan. **Rave**. 64p. $7.95.
- Day, Jean. **A Young Recruit**. 58p. $6.
- Di Palma, Ray. **Motion of the Cypher**. 112p. $10.95.
- Di Palma, Ray. **Raik**. 100p. $9.95.
- Doris, Stacy. **Kildare**. 104p. $9.95.
- Doris, Stacy. **Cheerleader's Guide to the World: Council Book** 88p. $12.95.
- Dreyer, Lynne. **The White Museum**. 80p. $6.
- Dworkin, Craig. **Strand**. 112p. $12.95.
- Edwards, Ken. **Good Science**. 80p. $9.95.
- Eigner, Larry. **Areas Lights Heights**. 182p. $12, $22 (cloth).
- Gardner, Drew. **Petroleum Hat**. 96p. $12.95.
- Gizzi, Michael. **Continental Harmonies**. 96p. $8.95.
- Gladman, Renee. **A Picture-Feeling**. 72p. $10.95.
- Goldman, Judith. **Vocoder**. 96p. $11.95.
- Gottlieb, Michael. **Ninety-Six Tears**. 88p. $5.
- Gottlieb, Michael. **Gorgeous Plunge**. 96p. $11.95.
- Gottlieb, Michael. **Lost & Found**. 80p. $11.95.
- Greenwald, Ted. **Jumping the Line**. 120p. $12.95.
- Grenier, Robert. **A Day at the Beach**. 80p. $6.
- Grosman, Ernesto. **The XULReader: An Anthology of Argentine Poetry (1981–1996)**. 167p. $14.95.
- Guest, Barbara. **Dürer in the Window, Reflexions on Art**. Book design by Richard Tuttle. Four color throughout. 80p. $24.95.
- Hills, Henry. **Making Money**. 72p. $7.50. VHS videotape $24.95. Book & tape $29.95.
- Huang Yunte. **SHI: A Radical Reading of Chinese Poetry**. 76p. $9.95
- Hunt, Erica. **Local History**. 80 p. $9.95.
- Kuszai, Joel (editor) **poetics@**, 192 p. $13.95.
- Inman, P. **Criss Cross**. 64 p. $7.95.
- Inman, P. **Red Shift**. 64p. $6.
- Lazer, Hank. **Doublespace**. 192 p. $12.
- Levy, Andrew. **Paper Head Last Lyrics**. 112 p. $11.95.

- Mac Low, Jackson. **Representative Works: 1938–1985**. 360p. $18.95 (cloth).
- Mac Low, Jackson. **Twenties**. 112p. $8.95.
- McMorris, Mark. **The Café at Light**. 112p. $12.95.
- Moriarty, Laura. **Rondeaux**. 107p. $8.
- Neilson, Melanie. **Civil Noir**. 96p. $8.95.
- Osman, Jena. **An Essay in Asterisks**. 112p. $12.95.
- Pearson, Ted. **Planetary Gear**. 72p. $8.95.
- Perelman, Bob. **Virtual Reality**. 80p. $9.95.
- Perelman, Bob. **The Future of Memory**. 120p. $14.95.
- Piombino, Nick, **The Boundary of Blur**. 128p. $13.95.
- Prize Budget for Boys, **The Spectacular Vernacular Revue**. 96p. $14.95.
- Raworth, Tom. **Clean & Will-Lit**. 106p. $10.95.
- Robinson, Kit. **Balance Sheet**. 112p. $11.95.
- Robinson, Kit. **Democracy Boulevard**. 104p. $9.95.
- Robinson, Kit. **Ice Cubes**. 96p. $6.
- Rosenfield, Kim. **Good Morning—MIDNIGHT—**. 112p. $10.95.
- Scalapino, Leslie. **Objects in the Terrifying Tense Longing from Taking Place**. 88p. $9.95.
- Seaton, Peter. **The Son Master**. 64p. $5.
- Sherry, James. **Popular Fiction**. 84p. $6.
- Silliman, Ron. **The New Sentence**. 200p. $10.
- Silliman, Ron. **N/O**. 112p. $10.95.
- Smith, Rod. **Music or Honesty**. 96p. $12.95
- Smith, Rod. **Protective Immediacy**. 96p. $9.95
- Stefans, Brian Kim. **Free Space Comix**. 96p. $9.95
- Tarkos, Christophe. **Ma Langue est Poétique—Selected Works**. 96p. $12.95.
- Templeton, Fiona. **Cells of Release**. 128p. with photographs. $13.95.
- Templeton, Fiona. **YOU—The City**. 150p. $11.95.
- Torres, Edwin. **The All-Union Day of the Shock Worker**. 112 p. $10.95.
- Tysh, Chris. **Cleavage**. 96p. $11.95.
- Ward, Diane. **Human Ceiling**. 80p. $8.95.
- Ward, Diane. **Relation**. 64p. $7.50.
- Watson, Craig. **Free Will**. 80p. $9.95.
- Watten, Barrett. **Progress**. 122p. $7.50.
- Weiner, Hannah. **We Speak Silent**. 76 p. $9.95
- Weiner, Hannah. **Page**. 136 p. $12.95
- Wellman, Mac. **Miniature**. 112 p. $12.95
- Wellman, Mac. **Strange Elegies**. 96 p. $12.95
- Wolsak, Lissa. **Pen Chants**. 80p. $9.95.
- Yasusada, Araki. **Doubled Flowering: From the Notebooks of Araki Yasusada**. 272p. $14.95.

ROOF BOOKS are published by
Segue Foundation • 300 Bowery • New York, NY 10012
Visit our website at **segue.org**

ROOF BOOKS are distributed by
SMALL PRESS DISTRIBUTION
1341 Seventh Avenue • Berkeley, CA. 94710-1403.
Phone orders: 800-869-7553
spdbooks.org